Head Start and Beyond

Head Start and Beyond

A NATIONAL PLAN FOR EXTENDED CHILDHOOD INTERVENTION

EDITED BY EDWARD ZIGLER
AND SALLY J. STYFCO

YALE UNIVERSITY PRESS   NEW HAVEN AND LONDON

Published with assistance from the foundation established in
memory of William McKean Brown.

Set in New Baskerville type by DEKR Corporation. Printed in
the United States of America by Vail-Ballou Press, Binghamton,
New York.

Library of Congress Cataloging-in-Publication Data
Head Start and beyond : a national plan for extended childhood
    intervention / edited by Edward Zigler and Sally J. Styfco.
    p. cm.
    Includes bibliographical references and index.
    ISBN 0-300-05685-0
    1. Head Start programs—United States.   2. Socially handicap-
ped children—Education (Elementary)—United States.   I. Zigler;
Edward, 1930–   . II. Styfco, Sally J.
LC4091.H43   1993
371.6'7'0973—dc20   92-26771
                                                          CIP
A catalogue record for this book is available from the British
Library.

The paper in this book meets the guidelines for permanence and
durability of the Committee on Production Guidelines for Book
Longevity of the Council on Library Resources.

10 9 8 7 6 5 4 3 2 1

This book is dedicated to Senator Christopher Dodd, in recognition of his indefatigable efforts in behalf of our nation's children and their families.

Contents

Preface and Acknowledgments

These are exciting times for everyone concerned about young children. Americans are rediscovering the importance of early childhood and are moving toward the view that high-quality care and education are every child's right. Policymakers have been quick to act upon these feelings by passing landmark legislation backed by substantial fiscal appropriations. Project Head Start has been almost unanimously declared a success and has been awarded the largest budgetary increase in its history. After years of effort by children's advocates, the nation finally has adopted a policy to improve the quality and quantity of child care available and to help low-income parents purchase it. In the last two sessions of Congress both houses passed a family leave bill, bringing us closer than ever before to a national policy that supports the pressing needs of families. Americans have often called themselves a child-oriented society, and these developments indicate that we are starting to justify that claim.

This aura of excitement about the early childhood years made a brief appearance once before, during the decade of the 1960s, when Head Start was born. We believed then, as we do now, that education is the solution to poverty and other social woes. If poor children could be helped to do as well in school as their middle-class peers, they could become more skilled workers when they grow up and be able to break the cycle of poverty. This was part of the reasoning behind Project Head Start, which was launched to provide comprehensive services to low-income preschoolers so that they would be ready to succeed when they entered elementary school.

The initial success of Head Start, coupled with a strong desire to improve the educational opportunities for poor children, soon led to other federal initiatives in schools. Project Follow Through was meant to be a large-scale service-delivery program that extended Head Start's effective model through the early primary grades. Title I of the Elementary and Secondary Education Act provided federal money to the nation's poorest school districts to improve the education delivered to low-income children from preschool through high school. With these three programs in place, it seemed that the nation had taken giant strides to better the learning environments of poor children so that they could eventually become contributing members of the society.

Over twenty-five years later, it is obvious that our efforts did not eradicate poverty or, for that matter, guarantee that all high school graduates could read. The three federal education programs still exist but have shown uneven rates of growth and success. Follow Through never became the national program envisaged and now represents a tiny experiment in education conducted in a mere forty schools throughout the entire country. As Doernberger and Zigler explain in chapter 2, some of the models have been quite successful, but dissemination of their methods is poorly funded, the program is far too small to make a difference in the lives of many children or the structure of many school environments, and the project has been threatened with termination so often that it is no longer taken seriously in educational and political circles.

In contrast, Title I (now called Chapter 1) has grown tremendously and now exists in over 90 percent of the nation's school districts. In chapter 3, Arroyo and Zigler describe the principles of the Chapter 1 effort and the procedures for awarding grants, but because individual schools use the funds at their discretion, there is no coherent "program" that can be articulated. Thus this massive and costly venture has not been systematically eval-uated. A generous interpretation of the meager evidence that does exist suggests that Chapter 1 services produce modest im-provements in achievement for some students. The basis for its growth and political and popular support appears to be that it has become a supplementary funding program for local schools rather than a demonstrably effective educational treatment (Carter 1984).

The bright star in the trio of programs is Project Head Start, the topic of chapter 1 by Zigler, Styfco, and Gilman. It has benefited millions of low-income children and their families over the years and has earned such widespread respect that legislators have authorized its expansion to serve all eligible preschoolers in the near future. And they plan to make it available not only to more children but for a longer period of time; the next step in the development of Head Start appears to be its extension into the elementary school grades through the newly created Head Start Transition Project. This latest effort is described in chapter 4 by Sen. Edward Kennedy, who introduced the legis-lation to establish the program.

The existence of these four federal programs shows that there is a genuine commitment on the part of Americans to help poor children succeed in school. They will spend nearly $9 billion on the cause—the combined budgets of the four—in fiscal year 1991 alone. But do the majority of Americans know what they are purchasing with this substantial outlay? Although most peo-ple are vaguely familiar with Head Start, both this and the school-age projects are not widely understood. The purpose of this book is to explain these programs—their goals, methods, and delivery systems—by tracing the history of each from its conceptualization through its current status. For the older pro-grams, evidence about their effectiveness is discussed and sug-gestions for improvement are made. Because the programs are treated individually, the chapters in this book are actually a collection of papers that, together, describe the major federal efforts to improve the education of economically disadvantaged children. The content of the papers necessarily overlaps, not only because the first three programs sprang from the same historical era, but because there is overlap in their goals and target populations.

In the final chapter, we take a harsh look at this overlap. Besides Head Start, we now have at least three federal programs in elementary schools for children who were eligible for Head Start or lucky enough to attend. The programs are anchored in different federal offices and departments and are authorized by different laws and subsections, but they all exist to do essentially the same thing for the same children. Despite their good intentions, lawmakers have promulgated different routes to the same end, crisscrossing for lack of an infrastructure. To eliminate duplication and better allocate resources, a coherent federal policy is needed.

We propose such a policy to meet the needs of poor children from the preschool years through the early elementary grades. By merging the four federal programs, we can structure a series of dovetailed interventions that appropriately address different developmental stages and together provide for continuity in the course of the child's development. By building on the strengths of each program while eliminating weaknesses, we can shape an integrated, sound intervention that achieves the goals that the individual programs have been less than optimal in realizing.

Our discussion does not include the many state and local efforts that have been quite successful in boosting school performance. (Some are described by the Council of Chief State School Officers 1988, and Schorr 1988.) Even Start, a new Chapter 1 effort to serve younger children as well as their families, is another promising development that is as yet too recent to assess. Such programs are omitted only because our purpose is to unify the existing national programs in order to make better use of the substantial federal sums now being spent. Our national plan does, however, incorporate elements of these successful projects. Its construction is built from the knowledge base in the field of early care and education, a base to which the smaller programs have contributed substantially.

We must warn that our proposal to consolidate federal intervention and compensatory programs is not a modest plan to be implemented after lengthy demonstration and evaluation stages. Some of our nation's lawmakers have a habit of being overly cautious when it comes to making changes in established programs or daring to try new ones. The Head Start Transition Project, for example, is being cast as a "demonstration program," although the concept has already been tried and proven by some of the early Follow Through models and similar private efforts. Even Start and the Comprehensive Child Development Centers are recent offshoots of the Parent-Child Centers that Head Start has operated since 1967 and the highly successful Child and Family Resource Program that it ran during the 1970s until the Reagan administration terminated funding in 1983. How many more times do we have to prove the effectiveness of these program types before they can move from the demonstration phase into wide-scale implementation to benefit more than the relatively small number of poor children who live near the model sites?

Apparently urging us to move in the *reverse* direction, Besharov (1992) has actually proposed "restarting" Head Start as a demonstration for two-generation programing. This suggestion implies that Head Start, a leader in experimenting with new ways to serve children and families, has learned nothing from its past successes and failures. Besharov's proposal also reveals that even this highly popular program is widely misunderstood. To set the record straight, Senator Kennedy replied, "Besharov is reinventing the wheel. Head Start is the pioneer two-generation program. . . . To veer off on such a tangent would ignore the benefit of two decades of Head Start experience and jeopardize the futures of millions more children" (1992).

After a quarter of a century of experimenting with methods

of early childhood intervention, it is certainly true that we do not need any more experiments. We have gained a vast amount of knowledge and it is about time we put it to use. Without further ado, we can write a coherent federal policy and mount an effective and comprehensive multiyear intervention that will benefit children and families today and for generations to come.

References

Besharov, D. J. 1992. Why Head Start needs a re-start. *Washington Post*, Feb. 2, C1, C4.

Carter, L. F. 1984. The sustaining effects study of compensatory and elementary education. *Educational Researcher* 13:4–13.

Council of Chief State School Officers. 1988. Children at risk. The work of the states. In Council of Chief State School Officers, *School success for students at risk*. Orlando, Fla.: Harcourt Brace Jovanovich.

Kennedy, E. 1992. Head Start in the right direction. *Washington Post*, Feb. 15.

Schorr, L. B. 1988. *Within our reach: Breaking the cycle of disadvantage.* New York: Doubleday.

Acknowledgments

Preparation of this book was made possible by the generous support of the Smith Richardson Foundation and the Spunk Fund. Claire Timme's able clerical assistance in preparing the manuscript is deeply appreciated.

Abbreviations

ACYF   Administration for Children, Youth and Families
BEEP   Brookline Early Education Project
CAP   Community Action Programs
CDA   Child Development Associate
CFRP   Child and Family Resource Program
DCE   Department of Compensatory Education, U.S. Office of Education
DOE   Department of Education
ECIA   Education Consolidation Improvement Act
EOA   Economic Opportunity Act of 1964
ESEA   Elementary and Secondary Education Act
HEW   Department of Health, Education and Welfare
JDRP   Joint Dissemination and Review Panel
JOBS   Jobs Opportunities and Basic Skills
LEA   Local Educational Agencies
NCE   Normal Curve Equivalent score
OEO   Office of Economic Opportunity
PAC   Parent Advisory Council
PAT   Parents as Teachers Program
PCC   Parent and Child Centers
PCDC   Parent and Child Development Centers
PDC   Project Developmental Continuity
SEA   State Educational Agencies
TIER   Title I Evaluation and Reporting System
USOE   U.S. Office of Education

Head Start and Beyond

Chapter 1 ■ The National Head Start Program for Disadvantaged Preschoolers

EDWARD ZIGLER, SALLY J. STYFCO, and ELIZABETH GILMAN

Project Head Start had its origins in an optimistic period of American history, a time when many believed that government should take a proactive, extensive role in eradicating the negative effects of poverty on children's development. Moreover, it was an era when it was popularly believed that the developmental course of children, including the growth of intelligence, could be vastly altered through timely intervention. Head Start became an instant success when early reports showed that poor children's IQ scores indeed increased during the preschool experience. When these gains were found to be short-lived, the program was nearly dismantled. Public favoritism was slowly rekindled as more sensitive studies began to show that Head Start did have positive, long-term effects on the child's ability to meet academic and social expectancies—a result of more practical consequence than IQ test scores. Today the program is once again enjoying enormous popularity and has been awarded substantial funds for expansion and quality improvements.

Americans' opinions of Head Start have obviously been characterized by very strong emotions. When they loved the program, they loved it too much and for the wrong reasons. When they hated it, their condemnation was too strong and again for the wrong reasons. The Head Start "lovefest" currently being staged in Congress falls into this same pattern (Chafel 1992, 9). In this chapter we trace the development of Head Start and separate the emotions from the evidence that forms the real basis for the program's support. We foresee some of the problems associated with rapid expansion and suggest a course of growth that begins with enhancement of the program's quality and services.

History of Head Start

In 1964, the U.S. Council of Economic Advisors reported that much of the country's poverty was contained in physically or culturally isolated enclaves in rural and urban areas. Half of the nation's thirty million poor people were children (Zigler & Muenchow 1992), and a large percentage of poor families were headed by a person with only a grade-school education (Johnson 1965). These daunting statistics were thought to be largely responsible for the rising crime rate and decline in the number of individuals physically and intellectually capable of assuming productive roles in military service or private industry. Political and economic conditions at the time gave both the desire and the means to mount an all-out attack on the problems associated with socioeconomic disadvantage. Through education and self-help programs, it was hoped, the War on Poverty could succeed in transforming the lives of poor Americans.

The Economic Opportunity Act of 1964 (PL 88-452) opened the war with three programmatic weapons: the Job Corps, the Community Action Programs (CAP), and VISTA (a domestic Peace Corps). The CAP were designed to assist local communities in establishing and administering their own antipoverty programs. Some local governments, however, opposed the CAP's proposed placement of administrative control and resources in the hands of poor people and therefore refused to apply for program grants. In an effort to make the CAP more palatable to local officials, while using what would have been an embarrassing budget surplus, the Head Start project was born. Sargent Shriver, head of the Office of Economic Opportunity (OEO) and chief strategist of President Lyndon Johnson's War on Poverty, envisioned an early intervention program as a way to "overcome a lot of hostility in our society against the poor in general and against black people who are poor in particular, by going at the children" (quoted in Zigler & Anderson 1979, 12).

Shaping an Intervention Program   A program for poor children was vaguely authorized under the Economic Opportunity Act (EOA), which mentioned that CAP should provide "a balanced program of educational assistance [that] might include . . . creation of, and assistance to, preschool day care, or nursery centers for 3-to-5-year-olds" (Senate Reports 1964, 20). But with the exception of a few experimental projects, there was little information available about how to meet the needs of poor preschoolers. Thus issues of program content, size, and duration were very much open questions for Sargent Shriver as he began piecing together a national intervention project. His first step was to appoint a planning committee of fourteen experts whose backgrounds were not only in early education but in child development, mental retardation, and pediatrics. This diversity ensured that Head Start would become far more than an educational program. (For a complete history of the development of Head Start, see Zigler & Muenchow 1992, and Zigler & Valentine 1979.)

Robert Cooke, the chief pediatrician at Johns Hopkins Hospital, chaired the group, which had only three months to develop their plans. The committee's recommendations, presented to Shriver in February 1965, were based on a "whole child" philosophy that embraced several areas: nutrition, physical and mental health, parent involvement, social services for families, and early childhood education. The goal the planners envisioned was to enhance children's overall social competence through the provision of comprehensive services.

The recommended components of the Head Start program were not especially unique, but never before had they been combined to form a multifaceted intervention. One element, however, that was virtually unprecedented in the design of preschool programs was the central role accorded parents. They were to be involved in the planning, administration, and daily activities of their local centers. One reason for this decision derived from Head Start's origins in the CAP, which were to provide self-help and empowerment opportunities to participating families. The planning committee was also influenced by the ideas of one of its members, Urie Bronfenbrenner, who was just beginning to develop his ecological approach to human development. Bronfenbrenner (1974a, 1979) argued that there is a complex interrelationship among children, their families, and communities, so that an intervention must touch all of these areas to be effective. This insight was an astute one: today, parent participation is recognized as crucial to the success of early intervention as well as later education (e.g., Powell 1982; Seitz 1990). Perhaps even Bronfenbrenner could not have foreseen how important the contributions of parents would soon become to the Head Start program itself. In that the first programs opened only a few months after the planning group made its report, parents were needed as staff members, a need they continue to fill. Parents also defended the program when its future was in serious jeopardy, so they are to be credited with Head Start's very survival.

Program Implementation   Expert advisers and planning committee members counseled Shriver that a small pilot program should be run and evaluated prior to mounting a large-scale effort. Yet the Johnson administration demanded that Shriver fire a major volley in the War on Poverty by beginning on a large scale, with at least one hundred thousand children. Both the president and the first lady liked the idea of a program for poor preschoolers, as did other lawmakers, professionals, and the general public. This popularity, occurring during a time of economic prosperity, propelled the growth of Head Start before it began. By the time the actual program was in place, it served more than half a million children the first summer (Richmond, Stipek, & Zigler 1979).

From the beginning, the basic Head Start program has been a center-based preschool serving primarily poor children aged three to five. Initially a summer project, Head Start was offered as a nine-month, half-day program in 1966. By 1972, most Head Start children were in school-year programs. Federal guidelines require that at least 90 percent of the children served be from families whose income falls below the poverty line; at least 10 percent of enrollment must consist of handicapped children. Head Start programs by law receive 80 percent of their funding from the federal government and the rest from other, usually local sources, which may be in the form of in-kind services.

Although many program variants have evolved from Project Head Start, the basic program is designed to meet the developmental needs of poor children in order to optimize their competence in social and school settings. Each program is required to provide developmentally appropriate educational experiences, health screening and referral, mental health services, social services, nutrition education and hot meals, and parent involvement. Although they must adhere to a body of national regulatory standards, individual projects are encouraged to adapt the program in response to local needs and resources (Advisory Panel for the Head Start Evaluation Design Project 1990). Thus it is somewhat misleading to speak of Head Start as a singular intervention because of the variety in localized programing.

Head Start as a National Laboratory   Head Start began as a hastily assembled but immense program built more on professional intuition than on scientific fact. The planners hoped their decisions would work out but were not convinced they had found the best solution to the learning problems of poor children. They therefore recommended that Head Start continue to experiment with intervention program development. Head Start thus became an evolving concept that spawned related efforts and illuminated new pathways leading toward the goal of better serving children and families. Some of these efforts eventually benefited families of all socioeconomic groups. For example, Head Start was instrumental in developing Education for Parenthood, a parenting and child abuse prevention program begun in 1972 for adolescents in schools nationwide. Head Start was also a pioneer in the grassroots family support movement that offers families from all walks of life help with personal problems through support groups and networks (Zigler & Freedman 1987).

The biggest portion of Head Start's experimental agenda has been to develop ways to serve very young children. Just two years after the program began, thirty-three Parent and Child Centers (PCCs) were opened to offer supportive services and parent education to families and children from birth to age three. This program is preventive rather than remedial in focus, aiming to reach disadvantaged families of very young children before developmental damage occurs. In 1973, seven of the centers were funded to provide child advocacy within their communities to promote better services for all children. The PCCs were the first program in the nation to combine the elements of child advocacy, community orientation, and family support.

An outgrowth of the PCCs were the Parent and Child Development Centers (PCDCs), a research and demonstration project begun in 1970 to study infant development and the importance of the parental role in that process. In the PCDC sites, models of family intervention were tested, varying with the perceived needs of the site participants. These programs were valuable laboratories for the development of sensitive service delivery systems that can be responsive to individual parents and children.

The notion of individualized services was coupled with that of continuous intervention in the Child and Family Resource Program (CFRP). The CFRPs provided parents and children from birth to age eight with a variety of support services (e.g., inoculations and health screening, child care, play groups, preschool) from which families could choose those they needed. The multifaceted nature and long-term commitment of the CFRPs was heralded by developmental theorists and social scientists and earned the praise of a governmental accounting group feared for its hardheaded scrutiny of federally funded social programs (Comptroller General 1979).

Head Start also began to experiment with ways to serve school-age children. Project Follow Through, instituted in 1966, was designed to continue comprehensive programing for preschool graduates from kindergarten through third grade. When it became clear that the program would remain a planned variation experiment (see chapter 2), project Developmental Continuity was launched to extend services and to coordinate the educational and developmental approaches of Head Start and the public schools (Valentine 1979). The new Head Start Transition Project (chapter 4) is the most recent attempt to continue services into the primary grades in an effort to sustain the benefits of the earlier Head Start experience.

Head Start also launched a program to address the national need for competent child care workers. The Child Development Associate (CDA) program provides classroom and hands-on training in meeting the developmental needs of young children. Graduates receive a professional CDA credential once they have demonstrated a number of performance-based competencies. Many CDA trainees have been parents of current or former Head Start children. The CDA program thus marked an important step toward ensuring that preschool education provided in Head Start centers meets adequate standards of quality, while helping parents improve their child-rearing skills and secure needed employment.

Evaluating Head Start

Head Start became a national laboratory for empirical research as well as program development. The program's uniqueness meant that standard design and analysis procedures were not readily applicable, and there were no assessment tools for some program goals such as social competence and parental involvement. Evaluation was made even more complex by the diversity of Head Start programs around the nation. Despite these difficulties, social scientists and eager policymakers wished to learn the effects of the project and began what unfortunately became, at least in the early years, a series of fragmented studies that were occasionally misguided in their approach to evaluation issues.

Early Studies   In spite of the many goals of Head Start, initial research focused almost exclusively on how much the program could raise children's intelligence test scores. This emphasis sprang from the mood of a nation infatuated with the belief that the environment could drastically alter the course of human development.

This naive environmentalism was rooted more in theory than in empirical fact. Prior to Head Start, Susan Gray and Richard Klaus (1965) had demonstrated that mentally retarded children could experience modest IQ gains from educational enrichment. About the same time, Benjamin Bloom (1964) introduced the idea of a "critical period" for intellectual growth. His research had convinced him that the most rapid cognitive development occurs during the first five years of life. He therefore reasoned that this period was the time when educational intervention would have its greatest impact. Another scholar of major influence was J. McVicker Hunt, who argued in his book *Intelligence and Experience* (1961) that the growing child's environment and the quality of mothering received were the primary influences on intellectual growth. He surmised that with the proper experiences, IQ scores could be raised as much as seventy points (Hunt 1971).

Given that much of the social science community had embraced both environmentalism and the idea of magical developmental periods, it is not too surprising that much of the early evaluative work on Head Start focused on intellectual gains. In the early stages, 1965 to 1968, findings tended to show that children experienced immediate IQ increases (Datta 1979), quickly bolstering Head Start's popularity. The praise was just as quickly withdrawn after the release of a study by the Westinghouse Learning Corporation (1969). The findings, showing Head Start's purportedly minimal influence on later school achievement and a virtual "fade-out" of the program's cognitive benefits, seemed to discredit the program's efficacy (Cicirelli 1969). Reactions to this report seriously jeopardized Head Start's future, to the extent that OEO considered initiating a three-year phaseout of the project.

Head Start administrators responded by sponsoring major reviews of the considerable research on the program that had been conducted by this time. One reviewer concluded that although Head Start did not produce permanent IQ gains, graduates appeared to have better social and academic adjustment in school (Ryan 1974). A review of much the same evidence, however, led Bronfenbrenner (1974b) to conclude that Head Start's benefits did fade away when children were in elementary school. He attributed the loss to the program's brevity and to the discontinuity between the program and the child's home and family experiences. Although he reconsidered his conclusion after the presentation of additional data, this report, coming from a well-known founder of Head Start, was more damaging than the highly publicized Westinghouse Report.

Critics of the Westinghouse study fortunately came to the

rescue. The report was attacked for problems with sampling procedures, statistical analysis, and appropriateness of the outcome measures (Campbell & Erlebacher 1970; Datta 1976; Lazar 1981; Smith & Bissell 1970). Theorists also began to take a more conservative view of how much intelligence levels could actually be raised (see Zigler & Seitz 1982). Intelligence came to be recognized as a highly stable trait, and the postintervention IQ gains were credited to improved motivation and test-taking behavior. A number of subsequent, more carefully designed studies revealed that Head Start's benefits are qualitatively richer and more durable than the first major report had suggested.

Longitudinal Studies Ironically, the planners of Head Start had never intended the program's focus to be highly improved IQ test performance. The original plans emphasized that Head Start's mission was to enhance the child's overall social competence, a construct that includes not only the elements of formal cognition and academic achievement, but also physical health (without which optimal performance cannot occur) and such motivational features as self-esteem and a sense of personal efficacy (Zigler & Trickett 1978). These factors can contribute more than IQ to an individual's ability to succeed in school and work and to become an involved member of society. In part because many of the elements of social competence are less amenable to study than the assessment of IQ, the question of whether Head Start and similar intervention programs can foster competent behavior remained relatively unaddressed until more sensitive longitudinal studies were undertaken.

Studies of long-term programmatic effects, notably that of the Consortium for Longitudinal Studies (1978, 1983), brought to light some of the benefits of early intervention in noncognitive domains. The consortium included a number of researchers who had evaluated eleven preschool programs during the 1960s and early 1970s. Insofar as was possible, the researchers located original program participants and collected a uniform set of information about their current status. Data from the programs were combined, but all significant results were reanalyzed by dropping the program with the strongest finding to determine whether it still held among the others.

The consortium results confirmed that children who attend quality preschool programs do in fact gain an initial boost in IQ scores that lasts for some years but eventually fades. The same held for reading and math achievement. However, lasting effects were found in other areas: participants were less likely to be assigned to special education classes and were somewhat less likely to be held back a grade in school. The rigor of the consortium methodology, and the findings of benefits that persisted in many children until they had reached twelve or more years of age, did much to restore public and scientific faith in the value of early intervention programs.

Other summary and longitudinal studies of Head Start programs have yielded similarly encouraging results. The Head Start Synthesis Project of over two hundred studies reiterated the loss of initial cognitive gains but reported on findings that Head Start children had better health, immunization rates, and nutrition as well as enhanced socioemotional traits (McKey et al. 1985). Family life was also found to be strengthened through the involvement of parents in the program. A study of thousands of children who had attended Head Start in thirty-three programs throughout Philadelphia showed that they had better school adjustment than peers who had no preschool (Copple, Cline, & Smith 1987). After at least sixth grade, preschool graduates had fewer absences, did not miss as many standardized tests, and seemed less likely to be retained in grade. Another large study of three groups of children who had attended Head Start at different times revealed that by the end of high school, the oldest group performed better academically than controls (Hebbeler 1985).

The longest-term and most famous study of the effects of early intervention is that of the Perry Preschool Program (Berrueta-Clement et al. 1984). One of the consortium studies, the Perry Preschool was created in 1962 by social scientists at the High/Scope Educational Research Foundation in Ypsilanti, Michigan. More than one hundred disadvantaged children attended a high-quality preschool program for one to two years, and their parents received weekly home visits to involve them in the educational process. The participants were found to be considerably more socially competent as they grew up than a comparison group. Social competence was measured by such indicators as high school completion, employment rather than welfare, and the avoidance of juvenile delinquency, criminality, and teen pregnancy.

The High/Scope finding that created the most excitement was the cost-benefit analysis. The investigators estimated the savings to society resulting from reduced grade retention, special education, and usage of the welfare and criminal justice systems, as well as higher contributions to the tax base resulting from higher employment rates. The analysis revealed that for every dollar spent on the preschool program, taxpayers received a savings of three to six dollars (Barnett 1985). This study helped to change public attitudes toward compensatory intervention programs: now they could be viewed as sound social investments rather than costly welfare projects.

Although it is somewhat difficult to extrapolate the likely effects of individual Head Start programs not included in the above studies—and indeed from the non–Head Start interventions—the salient effects of high-quality programs are sufficiently consistent to permit at least an inference of broad developmental benefit. By now, the accumulation of so much positive evidence has convinced professionals, policymakers, and laypeople that preschool services are a worthwhile cause. Recent legislation has granted Head Start the largest budgetary increase in its history, for the purpose of serving many more disadvantaged children as well as improving services. Should Head Start appropriations match the levels authorized by Congress, and be

put to the uses intended, the nation may re
a more accessible, high-quality Head Start p
the lessons learned from its twenty-five-year

Legislative Status

The alternating periods of favor and disfavor for F
have been reflected in legislation and appropriations o
years. With the passage of the Economic Opportunity Ame
ments of 1966 and 1967 (PL 89-794 and PL 90-222), Head Sta
became part of the strong EOA and was charged with creating
preschool programs to provide "such comprehensive health,
social, educational and mental health services as will aid children
to attain their full potential" (PL 89-794). In 1969, authority for
administering Head Start was transferred to the Department of
Health, Education and Welfare (HEW), where it would be nur-
tured in HEW's newly formed Office of Child Development.
Here Head Start warded off termination threats but barely man-
aged to sustain its funding level. In 1978, shortly after the
release of the consortium studies, EOA Amendments increased
Head Start's budget by $150 million. This was the first sizeable
increase and allowed the program to serve 376,000 children in
1980 (*Statistical Fact Sheet* 1980). At about this time attempts to
move the administration of Head Start to the Department of
Education were defeated by advocates, who feared the program's comprehensive nature would be compromised by the
more narrowly focused education establishment. In 1981, the
EOA Amendments were incorporated into the Omnibus Budget
Reconciliation Act (PL 97-35), and the program remained organized under Health and Human Services (formerly HEW).

The Human Services Reauthorization Act of 1990 (PL 101-
501) marked the most significant changes for Head Start. By
now convinced that early intervention could make a difference
in the lives of poor children, lawmakers authorized sufficient
funds to allow all eligible three and four year olds and 30 percent

ose not in kindergarten) to receive Head
4. Authorization was increased by $1 billion
fiscal year 1991; for 1992 through 1994, the
27, $5.92, and $7.66 billion. (Actual funding
these amounts for 1991 and 1992.)

grammatic changes include funds set aside for qual-
ements. In the first year 10 percent of the increase
lation, and 25 percent in succeeding years, is to be used
improving quality. Half of the set-aside is reserved for in-
ased salaries and benefits. Funds are also marked for training,
chnical assistance, facility improvements, and transportation.
Especially significant for enhancing program quality is the requirement that, by 1994, each Head Start classroom must have
at least one teacher with a CDA.

An important addition is the establishment of Head Start
Transition projects (see chapter 4) to provide supportive services
to elementary school children and their families, and to ease the
transition from the preschool to the school environment. Funds
are also provided to establish at least one Parent-Child Center
in each state to serve children under age three. Finally, and
perhaps most importantly for the continuing understanding and
improvement of program effectiveness, the recent act includes
authorization for a major longitudinal study of Head Start, research that scholars have long considered an urgent need.

The Race to Expand

As can be inferred from the scope of recent legislation, today
Head Start is enjoying nearly unanimous approval. Acceptance
pours out from the print media in such titles as "Everybody
Likes Head Start" and "Head Start Is One Program Everyone
Wants to Help" (Leslie et al. 1989; Rovner 1990, respectively).
A major national report prepared for the program's twenty-fifth
year was entitled *Head Start: The Nation's Pride . . .,*" effectively

capturing public sentiment (National Head Start Association 1990). Organizational supporters include not only professional education groups but the National Governors' Association, the National Research Council, the National Alliance of Business, and the Committee on Economic Development, to name just a few. Individual fans come from the ranks of the average citizen all the way up to the president of the United States.

Head Start now has so many friends that elected officials appear to be trying to distinguish themselves as the program's *best* friend by proposing to do more and more for it. Just as President George Bush offers a massive increase to the Head Start budget, half of the nation's senators join to cosponsor a bill to make Head Start an entitlement to all eligible children; the president soon counters with an even larger funding proposal. As "President Bush and members of Congress are waging something of a public relations battle over who is more supportive," it is hard to remember who came up with the idea of "full-funding," but it is now everyone's idea (Rovner 1990, 1191). These promises to give Head Start the money to attain full enrollment are becoming reality, and the program is now expanding at an unprecedented rate. In 1990 alone, Head Start added nearly 90,000 students, bringing the total to almost 541,000 enrolled (National Head Start Association 1991b).

The political bandwagon is only one of several pressures being exerted on Head Start to expand. For years the program has been able to serve only about 20 percent of families who meet the eligibility criteria. This injustice was generally overlooked until reports of the effectiveness of early intervention came to be widely accepted. If Head Start helps poor children, then they all should have the opportunity to attend. This is the thinking behind S.911, the School Readiness Act, which would provide annual billion-dollar increases over six years to make Head Start a universal program and steadily increase services for children from birth to age three. To date, however, no method of funding has been identified (National Head Start Association 1991b), so the "entitlement bill" remains more a vision than a plan of action.

Calls for growth in the Head Start program have also been sparked by federal mandates in the areas of human services and welfare reform. The Education of the Handicapped Amendments of 1986, or PL 99-457, essentially requires states to provide educational and other services to handicapped children between the ages of three and five, and encourages them to do so from the time of birth. The legislation itself was shaped partly on the basis of the positive evidence accrued from Head Start and other early intervention programs (Woodhead 1988). Head Start has been serving handicapped children since 1972; training and technical assistance have been developed for personnel in centers serving disabled children; and the position of individual case coordinator has been created to ensure that the needs of the child and family are addressed. In short, Head Start has the knowledge and experience to serve children with disabling conditions, and the states appear eager to tap into this resource as they strive to comply with PL 99-457.

The Family Support Act of 1988 may also have created some subtle pressure on lawmakers to increase the enrollment capacity of Head Start. The act created Jobs Opportunities and Basic Skills (JOBS), a basic skills education and employment training program for families who receive welfare. Participation will be required for parents whose children are age three or older. Like previous welfare reform legislation, the success of JOBS hinges on the availability of child care. The Administration for Children, Youth and Families (ACYF) and the Family Support Administration have been encouraging collaborations between JOBS and Head Start to supply additional child care slots, but few have been formed to date (Smith 1991). A similar role for Head Start may also be in the back of the minds of state officials as they begin to receive their Child Care and Development Block Grants. These funds are to be used to increase the quality and quantity of child care services and to help low-income parents purchase them—goals and groups with which Head Start is familiar. Although there is no formal link between the two programs, earlier versions of the legislation establishing the grants reserved a percentage of the funds for Head Start (National Association for the Education of Young Children 1990).

Another impetus to expansion are the national education goals adopted by President Bush and the state governors in 1990. The first goal is that by the year 2000, all children will start school ready to learn. Preschool training is the obvious strategy, and the majority of states have begun to fund prekindergartens as part of their public education systems (discussed below). Without a doubt, however, Head Start is the nation's tried-and-proven model for achieving school readiness. The program has been preparing preschoolers for elementary school for more than twenty-five years, and the evidence is convincing that those who attend high-quality Head Start centers are ready when they get there. This may explain why at least twelve states have opted to contribute public funds to their Head Start programs rather than initiate their own preschools. As minimal educational reform efforts are replaced by a thrust toward major restructuring of the education system, the emphasis on establishing preschool programs can be expected to intensify (Mitchell, Seligson, & Marx 1989). Head Start's position of leadership in this area has given it the status of a savior of sorts, adding to the factors that make a rapid growth spurt inevitable.

Misunderstandings about the Longitudinal Evidence

The expansion of Head Start is certainly justified by the large body of evidence on the benefits of quality early intervention. Yet many people have read too much into this literature, to the point that they view preschool education in general, and Head Start in particular, as the definitive solution to major national problems in education, business, and the social structure. A clear hint that popular emotions may be getting out of hand may be seen in the remarks of Gov. Neil Goldschmidt of Oregon: Head Start expansion would be the "most significant—and most effective—anti-drug, anti-crime, pro-education strategy" in America (quoted in Holden 1990, 1400). These high hopes ring back to the program's early days, when President Johnson announced that the summer Head Start program would be expanded to last for an entire school year: "This program this year means that 30 million man-years—the combined lifespan of these youngsters—will be spent productively and rewardingly, rather than wasted in tax-supported institutions or in welfare-supported lethargy" (in Califano 1979, 68). The promises of both leaders are a lot to ask of a program that is so brief in the life of a child.

Generalizability to Head Start Exactly how did Head Start "get the reputation of long-term life-builder and crime-stopper" (Holden 1990, 1401)? The main influence has undoubtedly been the highly publicized research findings from a handful of model experimental programs. The results of the Perry Preschool in particular have received so much publicity that they were referred to in virtually every recent document studied in preparation for writing this chapter. Such wide familiarity could indicate a field of well-read authors, except that in many instances findings specific to the High/Scope project were attributed to early intervention in general and, in some cases, to Head Start itself. Certainly most investigators have not found, or even looked for, the entire scope of outcomes studied in the Perry graduates. Yet we have read over and over again that preschool experiences reduce high school dropout rates, teen pregnancies, welfare usage, and juvenile delinquency. And no program has come up with the same cost-benefit amounts, but such undocumented statements as "For every dollar invested in child care for disadvantaged children, taxpayers ultimately save $7 in decreased expenditures for compensatory education, welfare and crime" are common (Florida Children's Forum 1991, insert). "Deservedly or not, [Head Start] has acquired a reputation as a program that is cost-effective" (Rovner 1990, 1192).

This aggrandizement might not have occurred if the media had given equal attention to the thoughtful analyses of the literature by Ron Haskins (1989) and Martin Woodhead (1988). Both reviewers took a close look at the consortium and other longitudinal studies on the effects of early intervention. They noted that both Head Start and the model programs produced immediate gains in intelligence, achievement, and socioemotional factors that dissipated within a few years. Haskins concluded that after that, there was very strong evidence that the models improved school performance, including less grade retention and special education class placement, but that the evidence for Head Start was only modest. Life success indices (avoidance of delinquency, teen pregnancy, welfare, and so on) produced modest evidence for the models but "virtually no evidence for Head Start" (278). This does not necessarily mean that Head Start has no such benefits, but that there may be little or no data collected about them. On the other hand, Head Start does have positive effects on children's health (Hale, Seitz, & Zigler 1990; Haskins 1989; McKey et al. 1985) and on the communities where they live (McKey et al. 1985), factors not studied for the model programs.

It should not be surprising that Head Start graduates fare less well than those who attended other, usually university-based programs. The latter were very carefully designed and monitored and had highly trained staff and substantial budgets for development and implementation. Head Start is delivered in nearly thirteen hundred places where it is tailored to local circumstances and quality ranges from excellent to poor. Yet Head Start is commonly referred to alongside the consortium and other projects "on the assumption that they share sufficient features" to produce the same results (Woodhead 1988, 444). This presumption is made despite the logical fact that it may be impossible to deliver on a large scale the intensive model programs that operate with considerably more resources (Barnett 1988). The per-child cost of the Perry Preschool, for example, was estimated to be $6,300 in 1986 dollars (Barnett & Escobar 1987), compared with Head Start's $2,767 expenditure four years later (National Head Start Association 1990). There is no way the national program could provide each child with the same level of services with less than half the money.

The appropriateness of applying non–Head Start evidence to Head Start has become the topic of a growing academic debate. Besharov has been particularly critical of the common assumption that Head Start produces the same benefits as model programs (1992a, 1992b; Besharov & Hartle 1987). He asserts that "not all preschool programs are created equal" (1992a, 521) and attributes to Head Start's "staunchest" advocates worries that "Head Start has serious problems . . . that often prevent it from making a lasting impact on disadvantaged children" (520). As will be discussed later, supporters *are* concerned about the program's problems, concerns centered not on weaknesses of design but on eroding quality. Their reading of the evidence is that high-quality Head Start services can indeed make a lasting difference. They note that two of the consortium studies were of Head Start (one extended by Follow Through) and that several of the others predated Head Start and inspired its planners. Instead of being irrelevant, "the results of these associated preschool research and demonstration projects tell us what is possible from Head Start" when excellence is maintained (Kotelchuck & Richmond 1987, 443).

It is a healthy sign that the academic community is taking a more critical look at the early intervention research. For some time experts apparently have been reluctant "to appear to be challenging the scientific base for politically precarious social and educational programs that achieve a great deal for children and families in poverty" (Woodhead 1988, 446). For example, relatively few analysts have pointed out that although preschool graduates surpass no-treatment groups, they do relatively poorly compared with the general population. In a study in Montgomery County, Maryland, Head Start graduates maintained their lead over a comparison group by the end of high school, but their performance was far below that of the middle- and upperclass students with whom they attended school (Hebbeler 1985). Among the Perry Preschoolers, over 30 percent were arrested at least once by the time they were young adults, and 33 percent dropped out of high school—results that may be unexpected in a report entitled *Changed Lives* (Berrueta-Clement et al. 1984). These facts should dim the oft-repeated claims that early intervention is a cure for such major social ills.

It is also about time that advocates face the sobering question of what can realistically be expected of a one-year treatment delivered at the age of four. Do we really want to believe that a year of preschool can ultimately shape the course of a human life? To do so is to ignore the many, many factors, ranging from the quality of schooling to socialization influences from the family and community, interacting and changing over time, that form the total environment in which the preschool graduate is raised. The effects of the intervention may survive as they proceed through these "transmission pathways," as Woodhead calls them, where they may be magnified or diluted along the way. It is shocking that so many have chosen to focus on a year or two when the child was a preschooler and have disregarded the many subsequent years of development, exalted a single experience over myriad others, and are now putting their hopes and money on early childhood programs as the solution—not part of a solution—to pervasive social problems.

If history repeats itself, this blind faith poses a significant danger to the very future of early childhood intervention. We saw what happened in the 1960s when there were ill-founded hopes, also based on model programs, that Head Start would permanently improve the intelligence of poor children. When this did not happen, the program was nearly terminated. Over-optimism can only turn into disappointment and jeopardize the object that failed to live up to unreal expectations. Another danger is that the current focus on the preschool years revives the infatuation of the sixties with magical periods in development. If we can just plug this or that experience into a certain time slot, the child will turn out fine. Development is a continuous process and, while it is important to give the child a sound beginning, that does not mean the future is secured. If all of the money and effort are poured into one stage of life, fewer resources will be available for other, equally significant stages.

Generalizability to the Present A different caveat beginning to be heard about the early intervention research surrounds its current relevance. The consortium and other longitudinal studies involved programs begun in the mid-1960s and early 1970s. This was a different era in American social history, a time of great optimism in the power of education to overcome the negative effects of poverty and in the power of poor people themselves to better their lot through self-help and political efforts. "[T]here is some reason to believe that family and community processes may have been particularly sensitively attuned to preschool effects at the time," so it may be improper to assume "that what has been achieved through preschool interventions with children born in the early 1960s would be reproduced in the same degree or kind if the experiments were repeated with children born in the 1980s or 1990s" (Woodhead 1988, 451). This argument is supported by Hebbeler's (1985) finding that children who attended Head Start in 1970–71 had better school performance than controls when compared in the early 1980s; this superiority was not found for the Head Start classes of 1974–75 and 1978–79.

Educational policies and practices have also changed in a way that may make some of the longitudinal findings obsolete. One change is the proliferation of preschool programs in the past two decades, which makes it difficult for researchers to assemble no-treatment comparison groups. In contrast, when Head Start began kindergartens did not even exist in thirty-two states (Zigler & Muenchow 1992), and opportunities for preschoolers were limited to private nursery schools for those whose families could afford them. Attitudes about the group care of young children are different now, and knowledge about their developmental needs has become more sophisticated—changes inspired to some extent by Head Start itself.

In addition to including younger children, school systems address the educational placement of older students differently from the way they did in the recent past. The emergence of "readiness" or "transitional" classes in the primary grades, and the increase in "social promotions" in later years mean that fewer children are held back and may be at least partially responsible for the steady rise in high school graduation rates. Thus earlier findings on the effects of intervention programs on grade retention and secondary school completion may not be replicable today. Similarly, comparisons of the academic performance of preschool graduates and their peers would be more complicated due to the widespread establishment of compensatory education programs. Finally, implementation of the Education of All Handicapped Children Act in 1975 has drastically altered the use of special education class placement, an outcome measure of the consortium and other evaluations. New referral procedures and mainstreamed classrooms gradually phased in as graduates of the consortium projects progressed through school, but if they were to start school today these practices would be the norm. All in all, changes in school policies "might alter, and possibly weaken, the measurable long-term impact of preschool intervention" (Woodhead 1988, 451).

The disadvantaged populations served by intervention programs have also changed over the years. Over the past two decades poverty has become more pervasive, there have been increases in single and teenage parenthood, and child and substance abuse have grown (see National Head Start Association

1990). The problems facing inner cities and impoverished school districts have also changed, further altering the environments in which young children are raised (Wilson 1987). No matter how ideal the methods of a model program conceived two decades ago, or how robust the findings of its subsequent benefits, it is an open question whether it would have the same impact today.

The fact that current social policies are being formed on the basis of old, sometimes marginally relevant data has been noted by several authors. During an ACYF research conference, "the lack of recent research was commonly acknowledged" (National Head Start Association 1991b, 35). The Advisory Panel for the Head Start Evaluation Design Project (1990) lamented that the expansive research on Head Start conducted over the past twenty-five years has not produced an organized knowledge base. While there is sufficient evidence that quality Head Start services have beneficial effects, attention to implementation is of relatively recent vintage. Head Start programs and populations vary from site to site, so those tracking the progress of graduates cannot assume they all had the same salutary experience or expect uniform outcomes to be achieved. We are reminded here of early research into out-of-home child care. Investigators initially asked the simple question of whether this experience was beneficial or harmful to children. Today they look first at the quality of care and then assess its effects on children of different ages, genders, and family backgrounds (see Zigler & Lang 1991). Until this more sophisticated approach is applied to Head Start, expansion will proceed without specific information about which program features work best and for whom.

Despite the need for a newer and better data base, those who have been close to Head Start over the years know that the program has immense potential when the services delivered are good. Head Start's growth and current popularity may be the advocates' dream come true, but these events pose another kind of danger. In today's climate supporters can become too complacent about the future security of early childhood intervention efforts. In the early 1990s no lawmakers and few scientists would want to be the only ones not applauding, but will this be true at the turn of the century? As noted earlier, historically Head Start has experienced periods of public enthusiasm followed by condemnation. Although its current status of approval has lasted for some time, support has been somewhat illusory. After the release of the consortium studies Head Start received its first substantial budget increase and was placed in a "safety net" where it would be spared spending reductions the Reagan administration imposed on most federal programs. Advocates settled back, believing they had finally won their case. However, cuts in programs that Head Start relied upon began to erode its ability to maintain services delivery even at previous levels (Washington 1985); and despite increasing appropriations, the average expenditure per child fell 13 percent in inflation-adjusted dollars between 1981 and 1989 (Rovner 1990). The message for Head Start supporters is not to rest on their laurels but to maintain vigilance, even though "Everybody Likes Head Start."

The Real Benefits of Head Start   Although there is little long-term evidence specific to Head Start, there are volumes of studies testifying to its short-term benefits (see McKey et al. 1985). Recent graduates do score better on intelligence and achievement tests, their health status is better, and they have the socioemotional traits to help them adjust to school. Some of their parents have learned to become involved in their children's education and have faith that their children will succeed. These factors may help them to be "better able to cope with the demands of schooling at a critical time when their identities within the education system [are] being established"; further, teachers may see the children as being more competent and their parents as more interested, attitudes that may "trigger a more positive cycle of achievement and expectation" (Woodhead 1988, 448).

These are certainly no small accomplishments for a program that, for most children, lasts only nine months.

The short-term benefits of the Head Start experience constitute the real support for the program's expansion and should not be underplayed. The findings are so plentiful and strong that it is perplexing why social scientists, pressured to "produce hard evidence on something everybody thought was a good idea . . . got pushed prematurely into looking at long-term consequences" (Ramey, quoted in Holden 1990, 1402). Rather than looking at whether Head Start can guarantee that a child will earn a high school diploma thirteen years later, or can dispel the temptations of crime over the life span, we would be better off studying how the very real benefits evident after the preschool year can be maintained beyond second or third grade.

It is also worthwhile to contemplate why preschool intervention is so valued for its potential future contributions, rather than for its current enrichment (Sigel 1991). Of course it is reasonable to assume that if Head Start raises children's social competence and improves some aspects of their environments, they might have a better chance to succeed in life. But by looking too far ahead, we ignore the here and now. Each year over half a million poor children and their families experience an improved quality of life, however fleeting, as a result of their involvement in Head Start. "A humane society need never apologize for that" (Kotelchuck & Richmond 1987, 444). This alone is enough to justify the expenditure; any longer-term benefits are a bonus.

Problems of Rampant Expansion

The preschool movement has taken the country by storm, spurring growth not only in the federal Head Start program but in the number of publicly funded prekindergartens nationwide. According to a survey by Mitchell et al. in 1989, twenty-seven states funded thirty-three preschool programs and twelve contributed to Head Start. Both types of effort typically serve four years olds, and, like Head Start, two-thirds of the state programs are for children deemed at-risk of having problems in public school. On the surface, the combined federal and state preschool developments suggest that universal enrollment will soon be a reality, and that the goal of having all children ready for school will indeed be achieved. However, the push to move and move quickly may result in programs that are not carefully planned and do not provide the quality that is absolutely necessary to produce benefits.

Head Start—and the nation's young children—have the most to gain or lose from the quickened pace of preschool growth. All early childhood programs are part of an "ecosystem," such that changes in one affect the other—for better or for worse (Mitchell et al. 1989). Rather than being complementary or supplementary efforts, Head Start and the state preschools are often parallel, if not opposing, forces. And common sense tells us that the program cannot make necessary quality improvements and accommodate surging enrollments at the same time. Head Start's success may have ignited the current preschool movement, but this burst of activity may be the biggest challenge the program has ever faced.

Competition with Others　As states continue to initiate prekindergartens in the public schools, and redirect education funds for school-age children to preschoolers, there is increased competition with Head Start for children, staff, funds, and other resources. Mitchell et al.'s analysis provides some telling examples. In Texas, school districts with at least fifteen children who are four years old and poor, or who have limited proficiency in English, must provide them with prekindergarten. As a result, Head Start has lost its space in some school buildings as well as some teachers. Because public systems generally pay more than the federal programs, their introduction of a preschool can drain the area of available teachers. For Head Start this can result in high turnover and leave less qualified personnel in charge. Instead of teaming up to coordinate programs, the new competition between Head Start and the public schools may only exacerbate historically poor relations between them.

Head Start and state preschools may also find themselves competing for students in some localities. It may seem premature to worry about this because Head Start is still some years away from having universal access. And it would not be a cause for concern if the two types of program were comparable. Unfortunately, they are not. One facet of Head Start that puts it far above the competition is the provision of comprehensive services. Only half of the public prekindergartens are required to provide services that go beyond education; few do so, and none approaches the level of services in Head Start (Mitchell et al. 1989). Even its educational component surpasses that of the state preschools in that it is more appropriate to the developmental needs of children at the ages served. Early childhood professionals fear that there will be a downward extension of the academic program from public grade schools to their nursery schools (see Kagan & Zigler 1987). "Without attention to the developmental nature of the programs offered, we do not believe they will work" (Farran, Silveri, & Culp 1991, 71). Yet public school programs may be a more convenient choice for parents than Head Start centers, in terms of location and transportation. Thus some children in need of full and individualized services may not receive them.

Both state and Head Start programs face additional competition from public and private day care services. Both types of preschool are generally half-day. About half of the families served by Head Start receive welfare (Smith 1991), and if they are forced to participate in JOBS their children may be unable to attend because of scheduling conflicts between work and school. Most state preschools also target poor families who will face the same problem. It is conceivable that many children who would benefit from early education will instead be placed in day care facilities that may or may not meet their needs. The child care system in this nation varies enormously in terms of quality, but the chances of finding affordable, good care are much less than those of obtaining poor care (see Zigler & Lang 1991). No matter how good the program at a public or Head Start pre-school, it cannot help children who are not there.

Endangered Quality   Head Start is not the perfect program, ei-ther as planned or as implemented in almost thirteen hundred sites nationwide. Over ten years ago the 15th Anniversary Head Start Committee, a major advisory panel convened to chart the program's future, pointed out areas that needed improvement and made recommendations for corrective action (U.S. Depart-ment of Health and Human Services 1980). Its successor on the twenty-fifth anniversary, the Silver Ribbon Panel, found many of the same problems were still present and had in fact worsened (National Head Start Association 1990). This is not to say that Head Start does not have many excellent programs, but that some are just fair or, unfortunately, poor. The national program itself has been struggling to upgrade and update its services in response to new knowledge and a changing generation of con-stituents. For these reasons, the quality set-aside in the Human Services Reauthorization Act is far more crucial to Head Start at this time than the money for increased enrollment.

Quality is threatened in all of the main service areas. Health and nutrition services are generally provided, but many centers have been hurt by cuts in federal food programs and community health care services that they relied upon. The lack of a medical director in the national headquarters leaves a void in leadership for this vital program component. Parental involvement and family support are the most neglected areas. In many programs there are no coordinators for either component (or for health), and these positions are often combined with others because personnel budgets have fallen short of inflation (National Head Start Association 1990). Recently over 70 percent of programs had social service caseloads higher than 60:1 (Chafel 1992). In the last four to five years, training institutes have been held in every area but parental involvement (National Head Start Association 1991b). The void is particularly worrisome because of general agreement that the benefits of Head Start are made possible by the involvement of the child's family, who support the intervention goals long after the formal program has ended.

Head Start's developmentally appropriate programing is also threatened by pedagogical and delivery problems. The planners left curriculum decisions to the localities, partially because the needs of their populations would vary from area to area. Yet the concept of "developmentally appropriate" has never been defined clearly enough to translate into specific educational methods (Farran et al. 1991). Quality of implementation essentially depends on local talent. At the most basic level the early childhood profession has come to agree that for a program to be appropriate to the developmental needs of preschoolers, class sizes should be restricted and staff/child ratios should be no higher than 1:10 (Bredekamp 1990). Although Head Start programs have generally maintained acceptable limits in these areas, there is concern that increased enrollment will result in larger classes with higher ratios. There are strong suggestions that quality deteriorates under such conditions (e.g., Whitebook, Howes, & Phillips 1989; Zigler & Lang 1991).

The biggest threat to the quality of Head Start is posed by staffing problems. Caregiver stability and level of skill have been identified as essential to quality care and directly responsible for positive developmental outcomes in children. In the National Child Care Staffing Study, quality of care was directly linked to staff wages and turnover rates (Whitebook et al. 1989). Low wages led to high turnover, which disrupted the continuity of the children's experiences and harmed their social and verbal development. In a nationwide survey of Head Start centers in 1988, Collins (1990) reported that teachers received an average salary of about $12,000, only 61 percent of the average compensation of teachers in public schools. In spite of poor salaries, Head Start has been spared high attrition apparently because staff are committed to their jobs. Collins found annual turnover in Head Start to be about 25 percent, considerably lower than that in other early care and education programs. Yet he noticed a disturbing increase in the last few months of the survey, suggesting that economic pressures may be beginning to take their toll on Head Start workers.

Calls to improve worker compensation have been made for some time (Chafel 1992; Collins 1990; National Head Start Association 1990; U.S. Department of Health and Human Services 1980) and wage and benefit increases have now been mandated in the Reauthorization Act. Although this is a promising development, current salaries are so low that it will take time for them to gain parity with other early childhood services and other professions that require educated workers. And although the act requires that by 1994 all classrooms have at least one teacher with a CDA, enrollments are increasing now. The need for additional qualified staff is immediate and may be difficult for local centers to meet.

Other quality problems exist in the areas of training, research and evaluation, and program oversight. Like the others discussed, these problems have developed largely because of inadequate funding. Statistics cited by the Silver Ribbon Panel prove the point: In 1990, the average cost per child in Head Start was far below the average in public schools and about half of what the National Head Start Association estimates as desirable. The cost per child *in constant dollars* declined by more than $400 between 1981 and 1989 (Rovner 1990). Research, evaluation, and demonstration efforts consumed 2.5 percent of the Head Start budget in 1974 but fell to .11 percent by 1989. Training and career development also experienced a decline. Program oversight has diminished considerably since 1970 even though the program became larger. Chafel (1992) adds that only one in five Head Start programs was monitored in 1988.

The best standards in the world are meaningless if no one is there to enforce them.

All of these difficulties compound to make Head Start less effective than it could be. The original planners had a vision of what every Head Start family should receive. Over twenty-five years later this vision is largely unfulfilled, and the addition of more children will only delay its realization. It is much wiser to serve fewer children well than to serve more children poorly, for the literature makes clear that only high-quality programs can produce meaningful benefits. For example, a review of studies led Weikart and Schweinhart to conclude that "only high quality programs consistently show success" (1991, 58). The first author testified before the U.S. Senate (1990, 49) that "Head Start is effective only when quality is high. . . . Below a certain threshold of quality, the program is useless, a waste of money regardless of how many children are enrolled." Head Start should be given the chance to correct its deficiencies while its size is still manageable, for they will only grow along with enrollment.

Making Head Start Better

There are clear ideas on ways Head Start could better serve children and families. Similar recommendations have been made for over a decade by "blue-ribbon panels and advisory groups of all philosophies" (Kennedy 1992), and these have been repeated time and again throughout the sizeable literature on early intervention. First, the program must last longer, and Head Start is now mandated to expend more effort in this direction. The Reauthorization Act requires that at least one PCC and one Transition Project be established in each state. These plans to expand services to younger and older children are based on the consensus of experts from many disciplines that one year is not sufficient to influence the behavior and attitudes the child needs to succeed in life.

Lawmakers' zeal for full enrollment may in fact thwart the realization of these long-planned efforts. There is no clear definition of what full enrollment is, and no one can say how much it will cost. Because it will undoubtedly mean a tremendous number of children and a huge bill for the deficit-ridden treasury, the Bush administration appears to be honing the limits of "full" to mean poor four year olds. It would further limit their Head Start experience to one year. Such an approach is one way to make limited funds go all the way around, but it goes against the wisdom of the field and shortchanges the participants.

Desires to add to the population served by Head Start have been voiced for some time, not only in terms of reaching more eligible children but of making more children eligible. Head Start has always been a segregated program. Although centers are permitted to open 10 percent of their slots to families above income guidelines, they must give priority to low-income applicants. Because it can serve only a fraction of them, the result is that poor children attend Head Start and wealthier children attend other preschools. Recognizing that this lack of integration cannot prepare children for the real world, both the fifteenth and twenty-fifth anniversary committees recommended that Head Start develop models for serving socioeconomically mixed groups.

Both groups also advised raising the income criteria to allow children just above the poverty line to benefit from Head Start. The official poverty index, based on food consumption standards in the 1950s adjusted for inflation, is terribly outdated (Urban Institute 1990). Nor does it consider differences in the cost of living in different geographic areas. The Federal Food Stamp, Medicaid, and Women, Infants, and Children programs have raised income guidelines in order to assist families in genuine need. Yet Head Start cannot serve these over-income individuals. Although raising the eligibility criteria to allow them access would be just, such a move collides with the goal of full enrollment. If Head Start were to adopt Medicaid guidelines of

133 percent of the poverty line, for example, an additional half-million children would become eligible (National Head Start Association 1991a). This would be costly and would delay the goal of universal enrollment. It is undeniable that many children of the working poor could benefit from Head Start, and that poor preschoolers could benefit from interaction with their more affluent peers, but recent expansion plans have not been drawn in these directions.

Other perennial calls have been to make Head Start more responsive to the needs of today's families. A common suggestion is for the program to become full-day, all-year in order to provide child care for working parents. This idea is now being taken more seriously because of the additional child care slots that will be required for the JOBS program. Today only a very small percentage of centers provide extended hours, although a new Head Start Family Day Care project is being implemented to test the feasibility of delivering services in child care settings. The Silver Ribbon Panel encourages Head Start to address child care needs but notes that many problems must be worked out in the areas of performance standards, materials, technical assistance, and funding. It appears that full-day services will take some time to be developed, but the consensus is that Head Start should move in this direction.

This is another intention that can only be delayed by rapid growth. The National Head Start Association (1991b) warns that the biggest obstacle to expansion is the practical matter of facilities. Between 1988 and 1991, the first year of phasing in full enrollment, more than eleven thousand classrooms were added. To find room for all of the children who will soon be enrolled, the association believes that home-based services or double sessions will have to be instituted. Head Start certainly cannot begin to meet families' child care needs if its classrooms are in use all day or if it must deliver the program in children's homes.

Many other long-overdue efforts to improve Head Start will be sidelined by rampant growth. Collins (1990) states that upgrade efforts, particularly increased salaries, compete with the goal of universal enrollment. So do suggestions to allow Head Start to purchase facilities so programs can have permanent, appropriate space rather than renovating or making do with leased or loaned classrooms (National Head Start Association 1990). Plans to strengthen the components of family support and parental involvement will not be achieved if the number of families to be served increases fivefold. Efforts to implement new performance standards that reflect new knowledge in the field and fill voids in the old ones will be put on hold; administrators will not have time to train and assist personnel in implementing new requirements if they are too busy adding names and searching for staff and space. In fact, soaring enrollments may force centers to compromise on standards for class sizes, staff ratios, and other components of quality preschool education.

Obviously, plans to improve Head Start have been under way for some time, and the importance of carrying them out cannot be overestimated. Quality improvements, especially the establishment of training and technical assistance and the Head Start Performance Standards, occurred in the early 1970s; in the synthesis project, studies conducted prior to 1970 resulted in smaller developmental gains than later studies, attesting to the positive impact of these efforts (Chafel 1992). In the early 1990s, the focus of legislative upgrade efforts is on staff compensation, hiring, and training as well as facilities and transportation. Yet to hasten universal access, the Bush administration has proposed restricting the quality set-aside to 10 percent of the budgetary increase, the rate authorized for the first year of the expansion but far below the 25 percent mandated in succeeding years. In the words of Sister Barbara McMichael, a Head Start director, "If we have to water down services to enroll more children, we will have accomplished nothing" (U.S. Senate 1990, 49).

Head Start is an excellent program in concept, but less than ideal in implementation. There is no doubt it should be available to every child who needs it, but not before it can assure them the quality services that are necessary for positive developmental outcomes. In planning the future of Head Start, the Silver Ribbon Panel listed the top priority to be ensuring quality, the same conclusion reached in other thorough analyses (Chafel 1992; Washington & Oyemade 1987). The panel adds a clear warning: "Program expansion should *never* occur at the expense of quality" (National Head Start Association 1990, 35). Quality improvements cannot be made overnight, nor should the program be expanded in the same time frame. Advocates must stop pleading for all of Head Start's needs and instead make some hard choices (Chafel 1992). Our choice is first to make every Head Start program a high-quality setting that guarantees known developmental benefits to every child enrolled and to his or her family.

References

Advisory Panel for the Head Start Evaluation Design Project. 1990. *Head Start research and evaluation: A blueprint for the future.* Washington, D.C.: Administration for Children, Youth and Families.

Barnett, W. S. 1985. The Perry Preschool Program and its long-term effects: A benefit-cost analysis. *High/Scope Early Childhood Policy Papers,* no. 2. Ypsilanti, Mich.: High/Scope.

———. 1988. "An economic perspective on preschool education." Paper presented at the National Conference on Early Childhood Issues, Nov. 18.

Barnett, W. S., & C. M. Escobar. 1987. The economics of early educational intervention: A review. *Review of Educational Research* 57:387–414.

Berrueta-Clement, J. R., L. Schweinhart, W. Barnett, A. Epstein, & D. Weikart. 1984. *Changed lives: The effects of the Perry Preschool Program on youths through age 19.* Ypsilanti, Mich: High/Scope Educational Research Foundation.

Besharov, D. J. 1992a. New directions for Head Start. *The world and I,* Jan., 515–31.

————. 1992b. Why Head Start needs a re-start. *Washington Post,* Feb. 2, C1, C4.

Besharov, D. J., & T. W. Hartle. 1987. Head Start: Making a popular program work. *Pediatrics* 79:440–41.

Bloom, B. S. 1964. *Stability and change in human characteristics.* New York: Wiley.

Bredekamp, S., ed. 1990. *Accreditation criteria and procedures of the National Academy of Early Childhood Programs.* Washington, D.C.: National Association for the Education of Young Children.

Bronfenbrenner, U. 1974a. Is early intervention effective? *Day Care and Early Education* 44:14-18.

————. 1974b. *A report on longitudinal evaluations of preschool programs.* Vol. 2: *Is early intervention effective?* Washington, D.C.: Department of Health, Education and Welfare (DHEW Pub. No. OHD 74–25).

————. 1979. *The ecology of human development.* Cambridge: Harvard University Press.

Califano, Jr., J. A. 1979. Head Start, a retrospective view: The founders. Section 1: Leadership within the Johnson administration. In E. Zigler & J. Valentine, eds., *Project Head Start: A legacy of the War on Poverty,* 43–72. New York: Free Press.

Campbell, D. T., & A. Erlebacher. 1970. How regression artifacts in quasi-experimental evaluations can mistakenly make compensatory education look harmful. In J. Hellmuth, ed., *Compensatory education: A national debate* 3:185–210. New York: Brunner/Mazel.

Chafel, J. A. 1992. Funding Head Start: What are the issues? *American Journal of Orthopsychiatry* 62:9–21.

Cicirelli, V. G. 1969. *The impact of Head Start: An evaluation of the effects of Head Start on children's cognitive and affective development.* Report presented to the Office of Economic Opportunity (Report No. PB 184 328), Westinghouse Learning Corporation. Washington, D.C.

Collins, R. C. 1990. *Head Start salaries: 1989–90 staff salary survey.* Alexandria, Va.: National Head Start Association.

Comptroller General of the United States. 1979. *Report to the Congress: Early childhood and family development programs improve the quality of life for low-income families* (Document No. [HRD] 79–40), Feb. 6. Washington, D.C.: U.S. Government Accounting Office.

Consortium for Longitudinal Studies. 1978. *Lasting effects after preschool.*

Final report to Administration for Children, Youth and Families. Washington, D.C.: U.S. Government Printing Office (Pub. No. OHDS 79-30178).

————, ed. 1983. *As the twig is bent: Lasting effects of preschool programs.* Hillsdale, N.J.: Erlbaum.

Copple, C., M. Cline, & A. Smith. 1987. *Paths to the future: Long-term effects of Head Start in the Philadelphia school district.* Washington, D.C.: U.S. Department of Health and Human Services.

Datta, L. 1976. The impact of the Westinghouse/Ohio evaluation on the development of Project Head Start. In C. C. Abt, ed., *The evaluation of social programs,* 129–81. Beverly Hills, Calif.: Sage.

————. 1979. Another spring and other hopes: Some findings from national evaluations of Project Head Start. In E. Zigler & J. Valentine, eds., *Project Head Start: A legacy of the War on Poverty,* 405–32. New York: Free Press.

Farran, D. C., B. Silveri, & A. Culp. 1991. Public school preschools and the disadvantaged. *New Directions for Child Development* 53:65–73.

Florida Children's Forum. 1991. Issues and action. *Child Care Focus.* Newsletter of the Florida Child Care Resource and Referral Network, Dec., Insert.

Gray, S. W., & R. A. Klaus. 1965. An experimental preschool program for culturally deprived children. *Child Development* 36:887–98.

Hale, B. A., V. Seitz, & E. Zigler. 1990. Health services and Head Start: A forgotten formula. *Journal of Applied Developmental Psychology* 11:447–58.

Haskins, R. 1989. Beyond metaphor: The efficacy of early childhood education. *American Psychologist* 44:274–82.

Hebbeler, K. 1985. An old and a new question on the effects of early education for children from low income families. *Educational Evaluation and Policy Analysis* 7:207–16.

Holden, C. 1990. Head Start enters adulthood. *Science* 247:1400–02.

Hunt, J. McV. 1961. *Intelligence and experience.* New York: Ronald Press.

————. 1971. Parent and child centers: Their basis in the behavioral and educational sciences. *American Journal of Orthopsychiatry* 41:13–38.

Johnson, L. B. 1965. The economic report of the president, January

20, 1964. In *Public papers of the presidents of the United States,* 164–65. Washington, D.C.: U.S. Government Printing Office.

Kagan, S. L., & E. Zigler, eds. 1987. *Early schooling: The national debate.* New Haven: Yale University Press.

Kennedy, E. 1992. Head Start in the right direction. *Washington Post,* Feb. 15.

Kotelchuck, M., & J. B. Richmond. 1987. Head Start: Evolution of a successful comprehensive child development program. *Pediatrics* 79:441–45.

Lazar, I. 1981. Early intervention is effective. *Educational Leadership,* 303–05.

Leslie, C., P. Wingert, H. Manly, & S. Hutchison. 1989. Everybody likes Head Start. *Newsweek,* Feb. 20, 49–50.

McKey, R. H., L. Condelli, H. Ganson, B. Barrett, C. McConkey, & M. Plantz. 1985. *The impact of Head Start on children, family, and communities: Final report of the Head Start Evaluation, Synthesis and Utilization Project.* Washington, D.C.: U.S. Government Printing Office (DHHS Pub. No. OHDS 85–31193).

Mitchell, A., M. Seligson, & F. Marx. 1989. *Early childhood programs and the public schools.* Dover, Mass.: Auburn House.

National Association for the Education of Young Children. 1990. *Early Childhood Advocate* 2(1).

National Head Start Association. 1990. *Head Start: The nation's pride, a nation's challenge.* Report of the Silver Ribbon Panel. Alexandria, Va.: Author.

————. 1991a. Press advisory, Dec. 2. *Outdated guidelines deny Head Start services to many poor children.*

————. 1991b. Washington update. 1990 Head Start funding and enrollment. Parent involvement survey. *NHSA Journal* (Fall): 22, 26, 30.

Powell, D. R. 1982. From child to parent: Changing conceptions of early childhood intervention. *Annals of the American Academy of Politics and Social Science* 461:135–44.

Richmond, J. B., D. J. Stipek, & E. Zigler. 1979. A decade of Head Start. In E. Zigler & J. Valentine, eds., *Project Head Start: A legacy of the War on Poverty,* 135–52. New York: Free Press.

Rovner, J. 1990. Head Start is one program everyone wants to help. *Congressional Quarterly* 48(16):1191–95.

Ryan, S. 1974. *A report on longitudinal evaluations of preschool programs.* Vol. 1: *Longitudinal evaluation.* Washington, D.C.: Department of Health, Education and Welfare (DHEW Pub. No. OHD 74–27).

Seitz, V. 1990. Intervention programs for impoverished children: A comparison of educational and family support models. *Annals of Child Development* 7:73–103.

Senate Reports. 1964. No. 23620, p. 20.

Sigel, I. E. 1991. Preschool education: For whom and why? *New Directions for Child Development* 53:83–91.

Smith, S. 1991. Two-generation program models: A new intervention strategy. *Social Policy Report* 5(1).

Smith, M., & J. S. Bissell. 1970. Report analysis: The impact of Head Start. *Harvard Educational Review* 40:51–104.

Statistical Fact Sheet: Project Head Start. 1980. Washington, D.C.: U.S. Department of Health, Education and Welfare, Office of Human Development Services, Feb.

U.S. Department of Health and Human Services. 1980. *Head Start in the 1980's. Review and recommendations.* Washington, D.C.: Author.

U.S. Senate. 1990. *Human Services Reauthorization Act of 1990. Report to accompany H.R. 4151,* Aug. 3. Report 101–421.

Urban Institute. 1990. Redrawing the poverty line: Implications for public policy. *Urban Institute/Policy and Research Report* 20(2):4–6.

Valentine, J. 1979. Program development in Head Start: A multifaceted approach to meeting the needs of families and children. In E. Zigler & J. Valentine, eds., *Project Head Start: A legacy of the War on Poverty,* 349–65. New York: Free Press.

Washington, V. 1985. Head Start: How appropriate for minority families in the 1980s? *American Journal of Orthopsychiatry* 55:577–90.

Washington, V., & U. Oyemade. 1987. *Project Head Start: Past, present, and future trends in the context of family needs.* New York: Garland.

Weikart, D. P., & L. J. Schweinhart. 1991. Disadvantaged children and curriculum effects. *New Directions for Child Development* 53:57–64.

Westinghouse Learning Corp. 1969. *The impact of Head Start: An evaluation of the effects of Head Start on children's cognitive and affective development. Executive summary.* Ohio University Report to the Office of Economic Opportunity. Washington, D.C.: Clearinghouse for Federal Scientific and Technical Information (EDO36321).

Whitebook, M., C. Howes, & D. Phillips. 1989. *Who cares? Child care teachers and the quality of care in America.* Final report, National Child Care Staffing Study. Oakland, Calif.: Child Care Employee Project.

Wilson, W. J. 1987. *The truly disadvantaged: The inner city, the underclass, and public policy.* Chicago: University of Chicago Press.

Woodhead, M. 1988. When psychology informs public policy: The case of early childhood intervention. *American Psychologist* 43:443–54.

Zigler, E., & K. Anderson. 1979. An idea whose time had come: The intellectual and political climate for Head Start. In E. Zigler & J. Valentine, eds., *Project Head Start: A legacy of the War on Poverty,* 3–19. New York: Free Press.

Zigler, E., & J. Freedman. 1987. Head Start: A pioneer of family support. In S. Kagan, D. Powell, B. Weissbourd, & E. Zigler, eds., *America's family support programs,* 57–76. New Haven: Yale University Press.

Zigler, E., & M. E. Lang. 1991. *Child care choices: Balancing the needs of children, families, and society.* New York: Free Press.

Zigler, E., & S. Muenchow. 1992. *Head Start: The inside story of America's most successful educational experiment.* New York: Basic Books.

Zigler, E., & V. Seitz. 1982. Social policy and intelligence. In R. Sternberg, ed., *Handbook of human intelligence,* 586–641. New York: Cambridge University Press.

Zigler, E., & P. Trickett. 1978. IQ, social competence, and evaluation of early childhood intervention programs. *American Psychologist* 33:789–98.

Zigler, E., & J. Valentine, eds. 1979. *Project Head Start: A legacy of the War on Poverty.* New York: Free Press.

Chapter 2 ▪ Project Follow Through: Intent and Reality

CAROL DOERNBERGER and EDWARD ZIGLER

What can be done to ameliorate the potentially devastating effects of poverty on America's children? For poor preschoolers, part of the answer has been Head Start. Shortly after the program's inception, the concept was extended to school-age children by Project Follow Through, a dovetailed program designed to serve Head Start graduates in kindergarten through third grade. Begun over twenty years ago, Follow Through shares Head Start's vision, but has taken its own course. From community action–based service delivery to planned variation experiment, Follow Through's intentions have been clouded from its inception, and while it is true that it has survived these past two decades, it does not share Head Start's esteem or its renown. Many believe that Follow Through has run its course and should be allowed to terminate. Others advocate the program's continuation, citing positive long-term effects for Follow Through graduates (Olmsted & Szegda 1987) and pointing to high levels of local satisfaction and parental involvement.

The purpose of this chapter is to inform the debate on Follow

The authors are grateful to those who so willingly shared their reflections on Follow Through. Richard Feldman and Eugene Ramp were particularly helpful in their comments on both historical and present perspectives.

Through's merit and its success as an early education strategy. Follow Through's history provides the backdrop for a discussion of the program's intentions, as recounted by planners, legislators, and Department of Education officials.

History of Follow Through

Detailed histories of Follow Through are presented elsewhere (see Elmore 1977; Haney 1977b; Kennedy 1977); the following historical outline serves to make clear the problems inherent in defining the program's purpose. Discerning the original intent of Follow Through is problematic because of two faults in its inception: the lack of time taken to develop and fully articulate the program, and the existence of two distinct program designs—large-scale service delivery and planned variation curricular study—that have never been reconciled.

Legislative Planning   Like Head Start, the evolution of Follow Through can be traced to the Johnson administration's War on Poverty and the passage of PL88-452, the Economic Opportunity Act (EOA) of 1964. Destined to become the centerpiece of EOA, Head Start was a clear expression of the belief that early intervention could compensate for the negative effects of poverty. From the outset, the preschool program was tremendously popular and enjoyed substantial political support. Government officials were therefore concerned when it was reported that the academic gains of Head Start children were nullified within months after entering elementary school. Sargent Shriver, then head of the Office of Economic Opportunity, or OEO, responded quickly to the perceived failings of the program. Rather than await further evidence assessing Head Start's effectiveness, Shriver called upon John Henry Martin and Jule Sugarman to prepare a speech for Shriver to deliver before the Great Cities Research Council in Milwaukee on November 18, 1966 (J. Sugarman, personal communication, June 12, 1990). This speech marked the birth of Follow Through, which Shriver dubbed "Operation Keep Moving."

Shriver introduced Follow Through as an effort to address the lament that Head Start gains were "crushed by the broken promises of first grade" (1966). The alleged fade-out of Head Start effects would be countered by a continuing intervention for program graduates from kindergarten through third grade. This initial conceptualization of Follow Through was virtually identical to Head Start in its comprehensive service delivery (including health, social, mental health, nutritional, and other support services) and emphasis on parental involvement. The close alliance with Head Start captured the interest of many, and Follow Through was to be ushered in as one of the last initiatives of the War on Poverty.

President Johnson urged Congress to support Follow Through on several occasions. In an address on children and youth given in February 1967, he specifically asked for legislation to implement Follow Through in the 1968–69 school year to serve 190,000 disadvantaged children (*Congressional Quarterly Almanac* 1967). Congress amended the EOA in December 1967 by enacting PL90-92, Section 222/a/ of which established Follow Through. The intent of the law is readily discernable: Follow Through was a programmatic mirror of Head Start, extended to children in the early grades of elementary school.

Conceptual Change   The congressional mandate came after planning and implementation of Follow Through were already under way. Follow Through was delegated by OEO to the U.S. Office of Education (USOE) almost immediately after it began (Elmore 1977); from there, Follow Through was assigned to USOE's Department of Compensatory Education (DCE). In March 1967 USOE and OEO formed the National Follow Through Advisory Committee and appointed Gordon Klopf as chairman. One of the authors of this chapter, Edward Zigler, served on this committee. At this stage of planning it was assumed that Follow Through would receive $120 million from the OEO appropriation in the fall of 1968 and that it would be implemented as a large-scale service delivery program at that time. Task forces within the advisory committee established guidelines for the program's personnel and staff development, guidance and psychological services, curriculum, research and evaluation, state assistance, family and community services, and health services (Rhine, Elardo, & Spencer 1981). Follow Through enrollment would consist of at least 50 percent Head Start graduates. Parent and community involvement were required; Parent Advisory Councils (PACs), made up of parents as well as community and school representatives, would be established in each local school district to give parents a voice in program governance and decision making.

Before Congress authorized Follow Through, a pilot program was begun in the fall of 1967 in forty school districts nationwide. The pilot was funded by $3.1 million from Head Start (Egbert 1981)—part of the OEO appropriation for 1967—which was awarded as grants to participating program sites (*Congressional Quarterly Almanac* 1967). The DCE administered the pilot, while OEO reserved the power to make major policy and funding decisions (Elmore 1977).

The participation of USOE was thus established early in Follow Through's history. Logistically it made sense because implementation would take place within the public schools. However, this shared responsibility between the USOE and OEO created difficulties in decision making and disparate interpretations of the program: the community action orientation of OEO programs was generally not appealing to the educational establishment (Kennedy 1977).

But discrepancies between the OEO and the USOE were not the major worries of Follow Through planners in the fall of 1967, for even as the pilot was begun the program's fiscal outlook darkened. The Vietnam War was fast eclipsing the War on Poverty in the minds of government officials and was placing increasing demands on the federal budget. At the same time it was suggested that a program of the intended breadth and complexity of Follow Through should be initiated on a small scale before expanding (Rhine, Elardo, & Spencer 1981). It became evident that funding would in any case not come through at the anticipated $120-million level; thus Follow Through planners met again in the fall of 1967 to reconsider the program's design. At this point the newly appointed director of Follow Through, Robert Egbert, suggested an experimental design involving planned variation and sponsored models to replace the fiscally impossible large-scale service program (Elmore 1977). Planned variation allowed Follow Through to survive in spite of a first-year appropriation of $15 million—approximately 13 percent of the expected amount.

The idea for a planned variation experiment resulted in large part from a growing alliance between social scientists and educators (Rhine, Elardo, & Spencer 1981). The planned variation design called for the concurrent implementation and subsequent evaluation of differing educational approaches in schools across the country. The approaches would be provided by sponsors—individuals, educational laboratories, universities, and private corporations—that were working on promising early childhood education curricular models. Sponsors bore the responsibility for model development, specification, and implementation in schools or program sites. Proponents of this method of social policy research saw Follow Through as an opportunity to gain valuable information on early childhood education on a low budget (Rivlin & Timpane 1975). The Bureau of the Budget (now the Office of Management and Budget) supported the planned variation concept as a step toward the utilization of rational choice as a basis for making social policy decisions, a move that would hopefully result in the wiser allocation of resources (Elmore 1977).

The full-scale program was thus put on hold, and Follow Through planners began to take steps toward implementing the planned variation design in late 1967–early 1968. Meanwhile, the pilot continued, based on the supposition that Follow Through would be a large-scale service delivery program. Following the dictates of the original executive initiative reflecting this goal, Congress passed the Follow Through legislation. But the direction taken after the planners' recognition of the funding situation was quite different than that of the program outlined in the mandate, which made no mention of experimentation, planned variation, or sponsorship.

The reasons for the lack of communication between Follow Through planners and Congress as to the new direction the program should take were largely political. Much of the appeal of Follow Through was predicated on its alliance with the popular Head Start program, and to represent it as different from Head Start—as a social experiment—was to endanger its political viability. Furthermore, while the decision to experiment was popular with USOE (Elmore 1975), Congress was interested in appealing to a constituency that wanted a community action program—not several different educational projects. Finally, many of those involved in Follow Through intended for the planned variation experiment to be a temporary arrangement to secure and provide information for its future once full funding became available (Rivlin & Timpane 1975).

The Program Begins   The establishment of Follow Through as a planned variation experiment began with the advisory committee's selection of model sponsors. Researchers who offered innovative approaches to early childhood education were invited to submit model designs to the planning committee for consideration; from these, twelve were selected. In early 1968, these sponsors presented their models at a meeting of personnel from ninety local school districts that had been selected as Follow Through sites. Forty of these sites had hosted pilot programs and were given the option of choosing a sponsored model or remaining self-sponsored. School personnel then had only until

September 1968 to familiarize themselves with their chosen model and prepare for the first wave of Follow Through children.

Follow Through, then, had experienced a metamorphosis in the period between Shriver's initial formulation in November 1966 and the start of the formal program in September 1968. The pilot phase had not been sufficient to establish the program: by the time the program began, it no longer adhered to the guidelines of the pilot, whose designers had no thought of planned variation experimentation. Time was not taken to test the program on a small scale, to conduct preliminary studies of each model, or to assess the problems inherent in implementing a community action/experimental program in the school system. Follow Through was forced to bypass the research and development, demonstration, dissemination, and implementation stages and begin at what is logically one of the last stages of program development, the field-test phase (Weikart & Banet 1975). Furthermore, the majority of the sponsors were rushed in their efforts to submit proposals, so that the models were not fully developed upon implementation (Elmore 1977). Sponsors Weikart and Banet (1975) summed up the experience of a Follow Through sponsor in the early phases: "The idea of planned variation may have been totally logical at the national level, but at the sponsor level it was mystifying . . . all created a feeling of bewilderment and even madness" (75).

The National Evaluation

With the decision to experiment, program evaluation came into focus as a major goal of Follow Through. The original plan was to assess five waves of children, as well as their teachers and parents, at the beginning and end of enrollment and at intermediate points (McDaniels 1975). By the time the final report was issued in April 1977 the cost of the evaluation had exceeded $40 million (McDaniels 1975), and difficulties had plagued it for its duration—many of them preordained by the program's hasty beginnings.

A lack of detailed model specification meant that the evaluation was reduced to a comparison of "black boxes": approaches that could be defined by overall philosophic orientation but not by detailed specifics (Anderson 1977; Rhine 1981a). It was thus impossible to determine what was being compared to what, especially in the early stages of the evaluation when the majority of the models were not yet fully developed (Elmore 1977).

Adequate measures to assess the diversity of the models' goals were not fully developed either. Conceptually, the models fell into three groups: product-oriented, which reflected a behavioral emphasis; process-oriented, dedicated to effecting lifelong change and boosting self-esteem; and parent-oriented, which focused on the active role of the parents (Kennedy 1977). The only valid and reliable measures available were cognitive tests, which favored the product-oriented models because they tested the behavioral products of short-term cognitive achievement and pencil-and-paper skills (McDaniels 1975; Rhine 1981b). Thus the evaluation was slanted toward cognitive effects, which did not fairly reflect the goals of all of the models (Bissell 1973; Elmore 1977; Hodges 1981; Rhine 1981b). Social scientists have questioned the solitary use of cognitive measures to assess the effectiveness of early intervention programs (Zigler 1970; Zigler 1990; Zigler & Trickett 1978), especially when evaluating a disadvantaged population (Bronfenbrenner 1976).

The evaluation was further hampered by the difficulties inherent in assessing differing models in communities throughout the nation. Classroom effects not only reflected the influence of the implemented Follow Through model, but were confounded by a host of local factors: the interface of each model with each particular school, the individual needs of the children and the community, and the skills and degree of cooperation of more than ninety different teachers. This diversity was exacerbated by the social service aspect of the program, which emphasized accommodation of the individualized needs of each child in each setting. While the proposed evaluation assumed the systematic variation of models, the Follow Through experiment was constrained by its preexisting design. The program was already committed to its original intent of service delivery and community involvement, and the decision to experiment was made with the awareness that the design could not disregard these considerations. Within each model, then, there was a high degree of variability between sites, and even between classrooms within sites, which rendered any intermodel comparison virtually meaningless.

Myriad other difficulties hampered the evaluation of Follow Through. The goals of the program as a whole remained ill-defined, as were the goals of each model (Rhine 1981b; Rivlin & Timpane 1975; Weikart & Banet 1975). The methods of implementation did not establish random assignment of sponsors to sites or of children to Follow Through classrooms (Kennedy 1977; Rhine 1981b). While random assignment would have been virtually impossible in such an experiment, its absence naturally compromised the results. A high rate of attrition affected many sites (Bissell 1973). Inadequate control groups weakened the evaluation design: control children often received benefits through Elementary and Secondary Education Act (ESEA) Title I, and in many sites Follow Through methods were adopted in non–Follow Through classrooms (Bissell 1973; Haney 1977a; McDaniels 1975). Thus most of the controls received some type of intervention, which weakened the comparison to Follow Through children. Implementation could not be assessed adequately because no measures captured the quality or the process of implementation (Elmore 1975; Rivlin & Timpane 1975). This was a crucial flaw, especially because the planned variation took place within established school systems, and a teacher's ability or desire to adopt the methods of the model clearly affected implementation. The alarming cost of the evaluation, together with its unmanageable size and scope, made it practically and scientifically unrealistic and required that it be reduced and streamlined as it progressed (McDaniels 1975; Rhine 1981a).

The importance of the evaluation in exploring rational choice in education (Rhine 1981b) was overshadowed by its failure to mesh with the original intent of service delivery (Haney 1977a). At a meeting of local and national Follow Through staff, sponsors, and evaluators in October 1968 it became clear that on the local level the program was perceived as a community action program that was incompatible with experimentation (Elmore 1977). Parents' discomfort with the evaluation stemmed from the perception that their children were "at the mercy of the experts" (House et al., 1978, 133). The evaluation rested on the hope that the sponsors would engage in collaborative problem solving to come up with adequate measures and make representative decisions, but acrimony and competition predominated instead (Elmore 1977; Rhine 1981a).

The evaluation began with children who entered Follow Through kindergarten in 1968: fourteen sponsors in forty-seven sites were included. When the data failed to show that Follow Through had produced the desired positive results—higher scores than those of the control group—Follow Through staff made the post hoc decision to call the first year an "implementation year," thus justifying public suppression of the results (Elmore 1977). Zigler has argued that this is the correct decision in this situation. The official evaluation therefore began a year later with the cohort that was entering kindergarten in the fall of 1969. Data were collected from eighty-nine sites representing twenty sponsors. But the data from this as well as the next cohort (children entering in 1970) were eliminated from consideration and were never publicly released: design and measurement problems wreaked havoc on data analysis, and the hoped-for wealth of positive effects did not materialize (Elmore 1977). The first analyzable data were those of the third cohort, which entered Follow Through in the fall of 1971. But at this point planners and evaluators, struck by the complexity of the data, attempted to simplify the evaluation by eliminating intermediate data collection. This reduced the cost and size but eliminated the evaluators' ability to assess the developmental effects of Follow Through (Elmore 1977). Even the scaled-down evaluation required literally ten tons of test materials, and a subsequent decision was made to evaluate only sites in major cities in the fourth year and to eliminate data collection on the fifth cohort entirely (McDaniels 1975).

Lackluster Results   Although the national Follow Through evaluation was haunted by design and measurement problems, the results do inform early childhood education, if not exactly in the manner intended (Hilliard 1978). The Follow Through evaluation report released in April 1977 highlighted three key findings:

1. There was a high degree of variability among sites within a model, but little difference among the models themselves.
2. Models that taught basic skills—the product-oriented approaches, such as DISTAR and Behavior Analysis—helped children to score well when tested on these skills.
3. Many models showed no difference between Follow Through and non–Follow Through comparison groups. (Brickman & Ramp 1987)

Anderson, St. Pierre, Proper, and Stebbins (1978) remarked on the poor performance of Follow Through children relative to grade-level norms.

Anderson (1977) put these findings in perspective by considering them in the light of four questions. The first addressed Follow Through's ability to raise poor children's test scores to national norms; results showed inconsistent effects. To Anderson's second question of whether or not the program raised poor children's test scores at all, the answer was, again, that it did so inconsistently. The third question was whether or not Follow Through at least maintained the children's scores at the level they would have been without the program; results showed a preponderance of null effects (67.6 percent) and a slightly higher percentage of negative over positive effects (19.6 versus 12.8 percent, respectively). Null effects are likely to be the result of poor comparison groups and implementation difficulties: if a model is poorly implemented then it will be little different from a comparison classroom. Anderson's last question concerned the existence of observable differences between the models. Reiterating the first key finding listed above, Anderson's emphatic answer was, "Of all our findings, the most pervasive, consistent, and suggestive is that the *effectiveness of each Follow Through model depended more on local circumstances than on the nature of the model*" (221). In effect, the idiosyncrasies of each site coupled with the service delivery goals of the program resulted in a unique model for every Follow Through site—even for sites sharing a particular model (Smithberg 1981).

The disappointing results of such a large-scale, premature evaluation were inevitable, according to Donald Campbell's (1987) reasoning in the broader context of intervention assessment. He advocates putting off evaluation until the program is "proud" of its accomplishments (347): only when a program claims success for itself is it likely to be judged successful by an evaluation. Evaluation before this point is likely to show poor results, as was the case with Follow Through. Campbell's observations are relevant to many problems that materialized in the first assessment.

Impact of the Results   As the national Follow Through evaluation approached completion, USOE regarded the program with skepticism and actively sought its termination. USOE had accepted Follow Through as a planned variation curricular study, not a community action–based comprehensive service delivery program; USOE officials were of the opinion that Follow

Through funds could be better used in supporting ESEA Title I activities, many of which targeted children in the same age range (USOE staff person, personal communication, June 1990). In the fall of 1972 USOE announced plans for the phase-out of Follow Through over the next three years (Elmore 1977; Kennedy 1977). Follow Through parents, however, rallied behind the program by protesting first to USOE and finally to Congress, where they were ultimately successful: Congress restored appropriations and renewed the program in 1974 (Kennedy 1977). But USOE remained unconvinced of Follow Through's value and continued to push for the program's demise. Following completion of the national evaluation, USOE in 1979 cited multiple problems in the program's organization and operation. The resulting recommendation was to direct 80 percent of funding toward direct services and 20 percent to program improvement (Rhine 1981b; Shive & Eiseman 1982).

In 1983, the administration of Follow Through was merged with that of Chapter 1 of Title I of the Elementary and Secondary Education Act of 1965 in the Division of Compensatory Programs. The program's diminution continued in 1986, when it was threatened with a merger of funds into the Community Services Block Grant, "a move that would effectively destroy the program" (Ramp 1986, 23). Again, however, Congress approved funding and extended the program.

In addition to reductions in size, development of Follow Through came to a standstill. Plans for follow-up evaluations focusing on model implementation and other areas related to the national evaluation findings (Egbert 1981; Gross & Gross 1982a, 1982b; Haney 1977a; Hodges 1981; McDaniels 1975) were never realized. Indeed, sinking resources into a program that appeared likely to expire at any time made little sense. This attitude was also responsible for a failure to redefine the program (Brickman & Ramp 1987), so what was to have been a temporary course of planned variation and sponsorship became the foundation of the program's organization.

The withdrawal of support by education officials is somewhat understandable. The original definition of Follow Through as a social experiment established the program as a short-term effort to identify effective educational models, not as an ongoing intervention strategy. Many believe it has already been extended far beyond what is reasonable for a demonstration program designed to develop and disseminate program models. Follow Through has never succeeded in reaching these goals, largely because the initial budget did not allow for full program development and the necessary funding was never forthcoming. Today Follow Through's $7.17 million annual budget is dwarfed by the $6.2 billion for Chapter 1. The USOE—now the Department of Education (DOE)—only begrudgingly administers the program (personal communication, DOE staff person, August 20, 1990). In spite of slipping through the legislative cracks into near oblivion, Follow Through continues to enjoy the support of Congress: the opinion of the constituency—that the program provides needed services—is apparently more salient than the empirical assessment provided by the evaluation (Haney 1977a) and the recommendations of education officials. One reason may be that the evaluation's quantitative results failed to reflect the more important qualitative results of the program (Hodges 1978; Hodges & Sheehan 1978). For many parents, school personnel, sponsors, and staff, service delivery has been and continues to be the focus and success of Follow Through.

Follow Through Today

Follow Through today functions on an annual appropriation of $7.1 million; it has remained at roughly this level since 1986. The current 14 model sponsors and 9 self-sponsored projects are represented in 40 program sites across the country (see table 2–1). These figures represent a markedly smaller program that it was at its acme in 1970, when Follow Through included 22 sponsored models in 173 sites spanning all 50 states, serving

Table 2-1. Follow Through Sponsors and Projects

Sponsor	Model	Number of sites
Model Sponsors		
University of Arizona	Tucson Early Education Model (TEEM)	3
Bank Street College	Developmental-Interaction Approach	3
University of Colorado	Inter-Reactive Learning Model (INREAL)	1
Fordham University	Interdependent Learning Model (ILM)	2
University of Georgia	Mathemagenic Activities Program (MAP)	3
High/Scope Foundation	Cognitive Curriculum Model	3
Illinois Renewal Institute	Cooperative Learning Model	5
University of Kansas	Effective Schools Approach (ESA)	3
Northeastern Illinois University	Cultural Linguistic Approach	1
Southwest Educational Development Laboratory	Language Development Approach	4
Temple University	Adaptive Learning Environments Model (ALEM)	4
University of Oregon	Direct Instruction Model (DI)	4
University of Tennessee	Cognitive Enrichment Network (COGNET)	1
Washington Research Institute	School Effectiveness Model	3
Self-Sponsored Projects		
Fall River, MA	Bank Street/Chapter 1	
Northern Cheyenne, MT	Behavior Analysis Adaptation	
Owsley County, KY	Child and Parent Project	
Macon County, AL	Child Development-Parent Interaction	
Hawaii	Development Interaction and Parent-Child Interaction	
Tama County, IA	Early Intervention	
Vincennes, IN	Individualized Self-Contained	
Puerto Rico	Open Block	
Goldsboro, NC	Responsive Early Childhood Education	

Source: The Follow Through Directory, 1990. More complete information on the models is available through the National Follow Through Association.

84,000 children (Hodges et al. 1980). The highest level of appropriations for the program was $70.3 million, also in 1970.

Follow Through continues to target Head Start and disadvantaged children: enrollment must be at least 60 percent low-income children and 60 percent from Head Start or comparable preschool programs (*Federal Register* 1989). Required services include (1) the implementation of an innovative educational approach; (2) parental participation; (3) demonstration and dissemination activities; (4) comprehensive services (health, nutrition, social, and other support services); and (5) parent and staff training. Follow Through is run as a full-day program, unlike ESEA Chapter 1, which most commonly pulls students from regular classrooms for intervals of remedial work.

Data on Follow Through's recent performance are scarce. With the exception of a study of parental involvement (discussed below), there are no large-scale evaluations. One reason is that the logistical problems of the original national evaluation have not been resolved. Another is the dearth of funding for and interest in a program expected to be terminated. There are, however, some small-scale studies, most of them performed by sponsors. These reports have revealed generally positive program effects.

In a study of the New Haven Follow Through (a project using the Bank Street model) Seitz, Apfel, Rosenbaum, and Zigler (1983) noted differences between Follow Through and non–Follow Through classrooms: program classrooms displayed an individual rather than a group-oriented approach, an interest in socioemotional development, and an emphasis on underlying principles and concepts. The Follow Through children were generally superior to controls in mathematics and general information but did not excel in reading skills. In a longitudinal, cross-sectional study, Abelson, Zigler, and DeBlasi (1974) confirmed the fade-out of Head Start effects in the absence of subsequent intervention and found consistently better performance by Follow Through over non–Follow Through children at the end of third grade. The gains of Follow Through children were commensurate with the duration and amount of effort expended in their program. In an analysis of longitudinal data provided by several studies, Olmsted and Szegda (1987) found that Follow Through students tended to experience lower rates of school dropout, grade retention, and subsequent special education placement than did comparison groups. In general, the authors found that Follow Through participation was a positive factor and that the specific model or sponsor was of less importance.

Although such findings reflect positive results in academic areas, the implementation of other aspects of the program is less clear. Some feel that, over time, curriculum has come to dominate program concerns and other components have fallen by the wayside (Ray Collins, personal communication, June 1990; Sharon L. Kagan, personal communication, September 1990). The program's continuation should be prefaced by its ability to fill its niche in early childhood education as set out in the mandate, particularly in the provision of comprehensive services, training, implementation of original approaches, demonstration, dissemination, and parent participation.

Comprehensive Services and Training Funding levels have drastically reduced comprehensive services. When pressure on Follow Through spending rose in the early 1980s, DOE reduced both expansion and support services; comprehensive services were the first to be cut (DOE staff person, personal communication, September 1990). In her survey of schools that were not among the initial program sites but later adopted a Follow Through model, Wang found that "almost half of the respondents claimed to provide no service other than instruction to students" (1987, 164). The schools that did offer additional services provided dental screening, health examinations, and nutrition instruction.

Parent and staff training has also suffered from funding reduction. While sponsors are responsible for training teachers in the implementation of their model, funds that once paid parents as paraprofessionals and classroom aides have essentially disappeared. Now there are on average 1.5 adults on hand in each Follow Through classroom, whereas once there were four (Eugene Ramp, personal communication, August 1990).

Implementation of Original Approaches   All sites adhere to a sponsored model or have developed their own self-sponsored approaches, but the value of Follow Through's sponsored-model approach is in dispute. When the evaluation found no inter-model differences, but rather stressed the quality of implementation, the importance of developing additional models was undercut. However, many are quick to point out that early education is in need of innovation and that what is learned in the demonstration of Follow Through models is important to the field.

Demonstration and Dissemination   Dissemination of Follow Through models can be informal, through the sharing of information between teachers, or formal, through the Joint Dissemination and Review Panel (JDRP), the National Diffusion Network, Follow Through Resource Centers, or direct sponsor-school contacts (Rhine, 1983). The latter occur when a non–Follow Through site requests model information from a sponsor. An example of this is the Follow Through project in Honolulu, Hawaii, which originally implemented the Bank Street model, then became self-sponsored, then disseminated the model to interested school districts on the outer islands (Rhine 1983).

As of 1986, forty-eight operating programs had been validated as exemplary programs by the JDRP; this is the highest proportion of JDRP-validated programs of any federally sponsored education program (Ramp 1986). Follow Through Resource Centers consist of program sites with JDRP-rated exemplary programs. When Resource Centers were established in 1978, twenty-two sites representing ten model sponsors were funded as Resource Centers, thus enabling them to disseminate information about their particular program. However, when their funding was cut from $3 million to $1 million in 1979, dissemination activities were curtailed accordingly (Shive & Eiseman 1982). Among schools that had adopted models through a Resource Center, Wang (1987) found generally high levels of satisfaction with their chosen program.

Parent Participation   Parent involvement has always been considered a key element of Follow Through. This emphasis is a direct result of the community action orientation of Follow Through's predecessor and initial program model, Head Start (Egbert 1981). Today most researchers agree that parent participation is beneficial in early education (Powell 1982; Seitz 1990). It has been acknowledged as an important force in school improvement and reform (Kagan 1989) without which intervention strategies are likely to fail (Bronfenbrenner 1976). Encouraging parents to take part in program planning and functioning is thought to enhance parental empowerment, the ultimate goal of which is to secure the families' independence from social support programs (Gallagher 1990). Parent involvement provides the link between home and school, a link crucial to developmental continuity and thus to the long-term effects of any early intervention program (Zigler & Berman 1983). When parents share in program planning, classroom activities, and learning at home, both children and families benefit, whereas the more common level of participation—semiannual parent-teacher conferences—does not in itself affect the outlook of the family or child (Gallagher 1990).

The EOA mandate of "maximum feasible participation" for parents allowed for a broad range of interpretation. Follow Through planners attempted to define their version of parental involvement more specifically, and the resulting language of the mandate was the strongest of any federally sponsored early education program: PACs, to consist of at least 50 percent low-income parents, would be involved with the planning, decision making, and operation of program activities (Keesling 1980; Rhine, Elardo, and Spencer 1981). In spite of this articulate definition, there is a high degree of flexibility in how each Follow Through site may meet the requirement. The activity and clout of each PAC and the overall level of parent involvement at any site are dependent on three main variables: the sponsored model, community characteristics, and school characteristics (Kennedy 1977). Furthermore, PACs are by definition advisory, not directive; mandating their existence does not mandate their effect.

Besides the PACs, parental involvement in Follow Through can consist of teachers reporting to parents on their child's progress, parent-teacher conferences, giving parents program plans and evaluations, and helping parents work with their children at home. More interactive involvement can take several forms: classroom participation (as aides, volunteers, or paraprofessionals), increased communication with educators, and educational opportunities for the parents themselves (Keesling 1980).

Historically, Follow Through has been successful in achieving parent participation. PACs have had a deciding vote in the initial selection of the sponsored model for their school, and in some program sites they maintained discretionary powers within their school district (Follow Through sponsor, personal communication, August 1990). The parent education model—no longer represented in Follow Through—boasted thriving parental involvement in the late 1970s (Gordon et al. 1979). Several DISTAR sites were protected from termination by active parent groups (Carnine 1979), and parent activism saved the national Follow Through program from extinction when the USOE moved to end it (Brickman & Ramp 1987; Kennedy 1977).

The last large-scale evaluation involving Follow Through was a study of parent involvement in four federal education programs, released in 1981. Five types of involvement were identified: governance, instruction (parents as aides, tutors, or volunteers), parent education, school support (noninstructional support of the school), and community-school relations. Although few cases of school change were found, positive personal outcomes (for example, parents' personal growth, increased knowledge about available services, and increased comfort with the school setting) were reported (Melaragno et al. 1981; Melaragno, Lyons, & Sparks 1981). The researchers noted a wide range in the nature and extent of parent involvement within each program (Keesling et al. 1981), thus reiterating the finding of high site variability in the national Follow Through evaluation.

Findings specific to Follow Through (based on the sixteen program sites included in this study) were that PAC attendance was generally low, that PAC membership tended not to reflect the ethnic mix within the program, and that key parents already tended to be involved with the schools in some capacity (Smith & Nerenberg 1981). If parent involvement has parental empowerment as its goal, then, according to these findings, PACs are not the best way to achieve it. Furthermore, although Follow Through guidelines establish PACs as governing, advisory groups, most PACs in the study focused instead on their role in parent education, noninstructive support, or school-community relations (Keesling et al. 1981). Despite these shortcomings in parent involvement, Smith and Nerenberg concluded that it is "alive and (in varying degrees) well in Follow Through, that it has real payoffs, and that others can learn from these 16 projects to enhance their own programs" (Smith & Nerenberg 1981, 237). Furthermore, the quantitative data capture only part of parent involvement; qualitative effects (such as parent satisfaction or community effects) are less readily portrayed by hard data. Thus a complete picture of the benefits of parent involvement in Follow Through may never be realized (Olmsted & Wetherby 1987).

Follow Through was organized to involve parents. But as funds to pay parents to work in the classroom have disappeared, so have the parents. Although grant size was found not to be a factor in the quality of parent involvement, at the time of the parent involvement study (now nearly ten years ago) several programs reported the need to cut or eliminate activities, such as services or workshops, due to funding cuts (Smith & Nerenberg 1981). In the ensuing years parent involvement in Follow Through has dwindled and represents "but a fraction" of what it was in the days of more generous funding (Olmsted & Wetherby 1987, 86). For example, the national evaluation reported that Follow Through parents were twice as likely to volunteer to work in schools as non–Follow Through parents (Hodges 1978), yet Wang (1987) found that Follow Through parents in her adopted-model samples were not significantly more involved than other parents in their children's classrooms.

Compounding the problem of involving parents in their children's education is the changing economic and demographic situation: many low-income children are parented by a single mother who must work full time and has little time or energy to devote to school activities. The ethos that supported activism and involvement in the 1960s and 1970s has also changed, and community action has waned in Follow Through as in the nation (Follow Through staff member, personal communication, August 1990). Actually, the association of Follow Through with community action has made its integration into the school system somewhat difficult even from the beginning (Planning Committee member, personal communication, June 1990). Then, as now, some school personnel felt somewhat threatened by the prospect of parent involvement, particularly in regions traditionally less amenable to activism (Elmore 1977; Weikart & Banet 1975). For all of these reasons, parent involvement in Follow

Through appears to exist on a site-by-site basis, moderated by the interface of school, community, and model characteristics.

Lessons from Follow Through

In the face of the nation's budgetary deficit crisis, Follow Through must be proven worthy of continuation as a federally funded early education program. There are some robust aspects of the program, and others that need to be reinforced to fulfill its promise. Following are some points that emerge from the present analysis and deserve careful consideration in early education programing.

Sponsorship   The sponsored model approach—the distinguishing organizational component of Follow Through—has lasting importance as an organizational strategy (Elmore 1977). Program implementation brought together sponsors, school personnel, and parents in a way not seen in any other federally funded early education program (Rhine 1981b). Beyond implementation, sponsors have a long-term role as a third party that intercedes in school-parent issues (Hodges et al. 1980) and are often the catalyst for parent involvement (Follow Through staff member, personal communication, August 1990). Sponsorship helps federal administrators run the program without controversy over local programing (Rhine 1983). Furthermore, sponsors maintain the link between practice and research (Wang & Walberg 1988), and their continued involvement enables them to revise their approaches as new findings inform the field of early education (Hodges et al. 1980). Follow Through's joint-grant funding structure ensures the sponsor's involvement, thus bringing together parties—researchers and schools—who otherwise would likely not communicate with each other (Follow Through staff member, August 1990).

The role of sponsors is valuable, then, for its potential to sustain the relationship between the participants and to keep local schools up to date on particular models as well as general educational developments. Sponsors are in a particularly good position to facilitate coordination of intervention efforts.

Coordination   Generally speaking, coordination among federal education programs and among the participants within a given program is rare (Crandall & Loucks 1983). Many researchers have commented on Follow Through's potential for improving this area, both by reducing redundancy of federal programs (Hill 1981) and by bringing together teachers, school personnel, communities, families, and sponsors (Rhine 1981a; Smithberg 1981). Yet little evidence supports actual reduction of redundancy, and levels of coordination beyond the sponsor-school link are difficult to define. Given the proven benefits of the sponsor's role in this area, Follow Through should assume the position of coordinator in the larger sphere.

Transition   Follow Through was designed to counter the fade-out of Head Start gains, yet little has been done to coordinate the two programs beyond mandating that 60 percent of the enrollment must come from Head Start or similar programs. The notion of critical developmental periods reigned in the early 1960s, but this concept was replaced by developmental continuity as the basis for optimal development (Zigler 1981). With the concern for continuity comes the emphasis on transition. Transition must involve the interaction of preschool and Follow Through staff and teachers to ensure continued support for each child, resulting in the interface of interventions (Zigler 1990). While Follow Through's lack of transition activity may be more indicative of problems between Head Start and the schools rather than program shortcomings (Follow Through staff member, personal communication, August 1990), the link between preschool and Follow Through must be strengthened if the program is to fulfill its potential as an effective early education and intervention strategy.

Much of Follow Through's inability to fulfill its promise is due to a lack of funds, yet Congress's repeated reauthorizations indicate that the social service goals of Follow Through are still viable. Follow Through's target population is in need of support in myriad ways. The program has not been *the* answer, but it has provided a valuable exploration of how to meet at least some of the needs of poor children. By capitalizing on the valuable aspects—mandated parental involvement and sponsor involvement—and compensating for the shortcomings of Follow Through by introducing additional programs or reworking existing ones, the field of early childhood education can surely be enriched. The move adopted by Congress that links Follow Through more closely to ESEA Chapter 1, thereby providing Follow Through with an arena for its models, is a step in the right direction. Follow Through must now strive to increase its transitional activities; to evaluate its efforts to involve parents; to enhance and expand the sponsors' ability to provide an interface between schools, educational researchers, and parents; and to make the best models available to more schools in need of their innovation, structure, and guidance.

References

Abelson, W. D., E. Zigler, & C. L. DeBlasi. 1974. Effects of a four-year Follow Through program on economically disadvantaged children. *Journal of Educational Psychology* 66:756–71.

Anderson, R. B. 1977. The effectiveness of Follow Through: Evidence from the national analysis. *Curriculum Inquiry* 7:209–26.

Anderson, R. B., R. St. Pierre, E. Proper, & L. Stebbins. 1978. Pardon us, but what was the question again? A response to the critique of the Follow Through evaluation. *Harvard Educational Review* 48:161–70.

Bissell, J. S. 1973. Planned variation in Head Start and Follow Through. In J. Stanley, ed., *Compensatory education for children ages two to eight*, 63–108. Baltimore: Johns Hopkins University Press.

Brickman, N. A., & E. A. Ramp. 1987. Follow Through: A brief history.

In M. C. Wang & E. A. Ramp, eds., *The national Follow Through program: Design, implementation, and effects* (Final Project Report 1:14–41). Philadelphia: Temple University Center for Research in Human Development and Education.

Bronfenbrenner, U. 1976. Is early intervention effective? In E. Flaxman, ed., *Educating the disadvantaged*, 123–48. New York: Arms Press.

Campbell, D. T. 1987. Problems for the experimenting society in the interface between evaluation and service providers. In S. L. Kagan, D. R. Powell, B. Weissbourd, & E. F. Zigler, eds., *America's family support programs*, 345–51. New Haven: Yale University Press.

Carnine, L. M. 1979. Parent involvement in education: The Follow Through experience. Paper presented at the annual meeting of the American Educational Research Association, San Francisco, April.

Congressional Quarterly Almanac 23. 1967. Ninetieth Congress. Washington, D.C.: Congressional Quarterly Service.

Crandall, D., & S. Loucks. 1983. *A roadmap for school improvement: Executive summary of the study of dissemination efforts supporting school improvement, vol. 10.* Andover, Mass.: The Network, Ltd. (ERIC Document Reproduction Service No. ED 240 722).

Egbert, R. 1981. *Some thoughts about Follow Through 13 years later.* Lincoln: University of Nebraska (ERIC Document Reproduction Service No. ED 244 733).

Elmore, R. F. 1975. Design of the Follow Through experiment. In A. M. Rivlin & P. M. Timpane, eds., *Planned variation in education: Should we give up or try harder?* 23–45. Washington, D.C.: Brookings Institution.

———. 1977. Follow Through: Decision-making in a large-scale social experiment. Ph.D. diss., Harvard University, Cambridge.

Federal Register. 1989. 34 CFR Chapter II, part 215, Nov. 1. (pp. 516–24).

Gallagher, J. J. 1990. The family as a focus for intervention. In S. J. Meisels & J. P. Shonkoff, eds., *Handbook of early childhood intervention*, 540–59. New York: Cambridge University Press.

Gordon, I., P. Olmsted, R. Rubin, & J. True. 1979. How has Follow Through promoted parent involvement? *Young Children* 34:49–53.

Gross, B., & R. Gross. 1982a. *Frontiers of research and evaluation in compensatory education.* Pittsburgh: Report of the Follow Through

Planning Conference "Documentation of school improvement efforts: Some technical issues and future research agenda" (ERIC Document Reproduction Service No. ED 254 337).

———. 1982b. *Towards improved compensatory education: Findings of five conferences to plan fresh Follow Through research*. Washington, D.C.: National Institute of Education.

Haney, W. 1977a. The Follow Through experiment: Summary of an analysis of major evaluation reports. *Curriculum Inquiry* 7:227–57.

———. 1977b. *The Follow Through planned variation experiment*. Vol. 5: A technical history of the national Follow Through evaluation. Cambridge, Mass.: Huron Institute.

Hill, P. 1981. *Follow Through and the problem of federal education programs*. Santa Monica, Calif.: Rand Corporation (ERIC Document Reproduction Service No. ED 244 726).

Hilliard, A. 1978. *The future of Follow Through*. Atlanta: Georgia State University (ERIC Document Reproduction Service No. ED 255 284).

Hodges, W. 1978. The worth of the Follow Through experience. *Harvard Educational Review* 48:186–92.

———. 1981. *Instructional models, model sponsors, and future Follow Through research* (Contract No. NIE-P-80-0177). Washington, D.C.: National Institute of Education.

Hodges, W., A. Branden, R. Feldman, J. Follins, J. Love, R. Sheehan, J. Lumbley, J. Osborn, R. Rentfrow, J. Houston, & C. Lee. 1980. *Forces for change in the primary schools*. Ypsilanti, Mich.: High/Scope Press.

Hodges, W., & R. Sheehan. 1978. Follow Through as ten years of experimentation: What have we learned? *Young Children* 34:4–14.

House, E., G. Glass, L. McLean, & D. Walker. 1978. No simple answer: Critique of the Follow Through evaluation. *Harvard Educational Review* 48:128–60.

Kagan, S. L. 1989. Early care and education: Beyond the schoolhouse doors. *Phi Delta Kappan* 71:102–12.

Keesling, J. 1980. *Parents and federal education programs: Preliminary findings from the study of parental involvement* (Report No. TM-6974/002/00). Santa Monica, Calif.: System Development Corporation (ERIC Document Reproduction Service No. ED 225 301).

Keesling, J., R. Melaragno, A. Robbins, & A. Smith. 1981. *Parent in-*

volvement in federal early education programs: Vol. 2. Summary of program-specific findings (Report No. TM-6974/005/00). Santa Monica, Calif.: System Development Corporation.

Kennedy, M. M. 1977. The Follow Through program. *Curriculum Inquiry* 7:183–226.

McDaniels, G. L. 1975. Evaluation problems in Follow Through. In A. M. Rivlin & P. M. Timpane, eds., *Planned variation: Should we give up or try harder?* 47–60. Washington, D.C.: Brookings Institution.

Melaragno, R., J. Keesling, M. Lyons, A. Robbins, & A. Smith. 1981. *Parents and federal education programs*. Vol. 1: *The nature, causes, and consequences of parent involvement* (Report No. TM-6974/004/00). Santa Monica, Calif.: System Development Corporation.

Melaragno, R., M. Lyons, & M. Sparks. 1981. *Parents and federal education programs*. Vol. 6: *Title I* (Report No. TM-6974/009/00). Santa Monica, Calif.: System Develpment Corporation.

Olmsted, P. P., & M. J. Szegda. 1987. Long-term effects of Follow Through participation. In M. Wang & E. Ramp, eds., *The national Follow Through program: Design, implementation, and effects* (Final project report 1:92–110). Philadelphia: Temple University Center for Research in Human Development and Education.

Olmsted, P. P., & M. J. Wetherby. 1987. Parent involvement in the Follow Through program. In M. Wang & E. Ramp, eds., *The national Follow Through program: Design, implementation, and effects* (Final project report 1:65–91). Philadelphia: Temple University Center for Research in Human Development and Education.

Powell, D. R. 1982. From child to parent: Changing conceptions of early childhood intervention. *Annals of the American Academy of Politics and Social Science* 461:135–44.

Ramp, E. A. 1986. [Written testimony]. *Reauthorization of the Follow Through program* (Hearing Report, Serial No. 99–103, pp. 1–25), Feb. 20. Washington, D.C.: U.S. Government Printing Office.

Rhine, W. R. 1981a. An overview. In W. R. Rhine, ed., *Making schools more effective: New directions from Follow Through*, 3–24. New York: Academic Press.

———. 1981b. Follow Through: Perspectives and possibilities. In W. R. Rhine, ed., *Making schools more effective: New directions from Follow Through*, 291–324. New York: Academic Press.

———. 1983. The role of psychologists in the national Follow Through project. *American Psychologist* 38:288–97.

Rhine, W. R., R. Elardo, & L. M. Spencer. 1981. Improving educational environments: The Follow Through approach. In W. R. Rhine, ed., *Making schools more effective: New directions from Follow Through*, 25–46. New York: Academic Press.

Rivlin, A. M., & P. M. Timpane. 1975. Planned variation in education: An assessment. In A. M. Rivlin & P. M. Timpane, eds., *Planned variation: Should we give up or try harder?* 1–21. Washington, D.C.: Brookings Institution.

Seitz, V. 1990. Intervention programs for impoverished children: A comparison of education and family support models. *Annals of Child Development* 7:73–103.

Seitz, V., N. H. Apfel, L. K. Rosenbaum, & E. Zigler. 1983. Long-term effects of projects Head Start and Follow Through: The New Haven project. In Consortium for Longitudinal Studies, ed., *As the twig is bent: Lasting effects of preschool programs*, 299–332. Hillsdale, N.J.: Erlbaum.

Shive, G., & J. Eiseman. 1982. *Dissemination for school improvement: An analysis of nine federal education programs*. Andover, Mass.: Network of Innovative Schools, Inc. (ERIC Document Reproduction Services No. ED 240 717).

Shriver, S. 1966. Speech delivered before the Great Cities Research Council, Milwaukee, Nov. 18.

Smith, A. G., & S. Nerenberg. 1981. *Parents and federal early education programs*. Vol. 5: *Follow Through* (Report No. TM-6974/008/00). Santa Monica, Calif.: System Development Corporation.

Smithberg, L. 1981. *Follow Through: Illusion and paradox in educational experimentation*. Washington, D.C.: National Institute of Education (ERIC Document Reproduction Service No. ED 245 793).

Wang, M. C. 1987. An analysis of the impact of the dissemination component of the national Follow Through program. In M. Wang & E. Ramp, eds., *The national Follow Through program: Design, implementation, and effects* (Final Project Report 1:153–96). Philadelphia: Temple University Center for Research in Human Development and Education.

Wang, M. C., & H. Walberg. 1988. *The national Follow Through program: Lessons from two decades of research and practice in school improvement*. Philadelphia: Temple University Center for Research in Human Development and Education.

Weikart, D. P., & A. Banet. 1975. Model design problems in Follow

Through. In A. M. Rivlin & P. M. Timpane, eds., *Planned variation: Should we give up or try harder?* 61–77. Washington, D.C.: Brookings Institution.

Wolff, M., & A. Stein. 1967. Head Start six months later. *Phi Delta Kappan* 48:349–50.

Zigler, E. 1970. The environmental mystique: Training the intellect versus development of the child. *Childhood Education* 46:402–12.

———. 1981. Foreword. In W. R. Rhine, ed., *Making schools more effective: New directions from Follow Through*, 3–24. New York: Academic Press.

———. 1990. Foreword. In S. J. Meisels & J. P. Shonkoff, eds., *Handbook of early childhood intervention*, ix–xiv. New York: Cambridge University Press.

Zigler, E., & W. Berman. 1983. Discerning the future of early childhood intervention. *American Psychologist* 38:894–906.

Zigler, E., & P. Trickett. 1978. IQ, social competence, and evaluation of early childhood intervention programs. *American Psychologist* 33:789–98.

Chapter 3 ■ America's Title I/Chapter I Programs: Why the Promise Has Not Been Met

CARMEN G. ARROYO and EDWARD ZIGLER

Title I of the Elementary and Secondary Education Act of 1965 (ESEA) was passed to provide federal financial assistance to local education agencies to improve services for "educationally deprived," low-income children. President Lyndon B. Johnson believed that the act would "bring better education to millions of disadvantaged youth who need it most" and that schools would become "the vital factor in breaking the cycle of poverty" (S. REP. No. 146, p. 1450). On signing the ESEA, Johnson said, "I believe no law I have signed, or will ever sign, means more to the future of America" (cited in S. REP. No. 726, p. 2736). These words were indeed prophetic. Although Title I of ESEA has undergone numerous changes, no other piece of legislation in American history has been so influential in shaping the way our nation's schools address the needs of poor, low-achieving children.

According to the most recent estimates, federal compensatory education funds reach 90 percent of the nation's school districts (Birman et al. 1987; Sinclair & Guttman 1990; S. REP. No. 222). During the 1990–91 academic school year, the federal government spent approximately $5 billion on Title I (now called Chapter 1) education services for an estimated five million school-children (U.S. Department of Education 1990b). For 1991–92, the budget increased substantially to $6.2 billion. During fiscal year 1989, the $4.6 billion (National Center for Education Statistics 1989) allotted to Chapter 1 represented 20 percent of the federal funds for programs administered by the Department of Education, and 75 percent of the department's total budget for use in elementary and secondary schools.

Although Title I receives a significant portion of federal expenditures for education, over the past twenty-five years Title I services have produced only small changes in the educational attainment of economically disadvantaged children. Despite these modest effects, support for the program is quite strong. In 1989, the Senate approved the reauthorization for Title I/Chapter 1 by a vote of ninety-seven to one while the House passed it with only one dissenting voice (Ralph 1989). Title I/Chapter 1 also receives overwhelming support from state and local agencies, teachers, principals, academic researchers, and policy analysts (Plunkett 1985; Ralph 1989). It has been argued that such support in the face of little positive evidence reflects diminished expectations for compensatory education programs (Jencks 1986; Ralph 1989). Because the effects of compensatory programs are modest and ephemeral, evaluators have forsaken the program's original lofty goals and view Chapter 1 simply as a funding source for disadvantaged students (Carter 1984; Ralph 1989).

Title I's failures to "break the cycle of poverty" can be attributed to the tremendous variability in the way program funds are applied in thousands of schools across the country. Yet this variability—if clarified—is potentially the program's strongest feature. Title I's sensitivity to the individual needs of the children and localities served must be retained, but the program's goals and targeting practices must be reexamined. With greater specification, Title I can rightfully gain a place in the experimenting society envisioned by Donald Campbell, former president of the American Psychological Association.

In 1968 Campbell recommended that the United States adopt an experimental approach to social reform that emulated the methodology of the social sciences. He envisioned a nation prepared to "try out new programs designed to cure specific social problems, in which we learn whether or not these programs are effective, and in which we retain, imitate, modify, or discard them on the basis of apparent effectiveness" (1969, 409). Title I has certainly been a social experiment that has shaped the nation's definitions of the structure and purpose of compensatory education. However, the experiment appears to have stopped at the implementation stage. Policymakers and planners have not applied to Title I services Campbell's recommendations that programs be continually assessed, modified, or eliminated on the basis of their effectiveness. Subsequent amendments to Title I have focused primarily on issues related to administration with little attention being given to program evaluation and improvement.

In the following discussion, a brief history of Title I will be presented. The goals and framework of compensatory education as outlined by Title I will be discussed, and the implications of Title I policies on researchers' ability to plan, implement, and evaluate federally sponsored compensatory education programs will be analyzed. The full history and structure of federal education legislation are quite complex, and an exhaustive description of Title I's many features is beyond the scope of this chapter. We therefore highlight only the aspects of the legislation that are most relevant to our understanding of the relationship between the conceptual framework of federal education policies and their implementation and formal evaluation.

The Rise of Federal Compensatory Education Services

Although the 1960s were a time of economic prosperity for the majority of Americans, the appraisals of social scientists (Harrington 1962) and a study undertaken by the Kennedy administration (President's Panel on Mental Retardation, cited in Zigler & Freedman 1987) cautioned that the nation's social and economic well-being was continually threatened by the inferior living conditions and patterns evident among the minority of people who were economically or "culturally" deprived. The inability of large numbers of draftees to read or write at the eighth-grade level, the high percentage of adults who did not complete a high school education, the expense of employment training, and the high unemployment rate among the nation's eighteen- to twenty-four-year-olds compelled President Johnson to call for greater federal intervention to resolve the "national problem" of educational and occupational unpreparedness (S. REP. No. 146). In the view of the Johnson administration, a federal war against all social factors detrimental to American stability and prosperity was needed.

The War on Poverty declared by Johnson in 1964 embodied a basic belief that education and self-determination would improve the economic and social conditions of the nation's impoverished citizens. While many programs developed under the war's declaration (the Economic Opportunity Act of 1964) focused primarily on the needs of adults and communities, policies to meet the specific needs of children also evolved from the reformist philosophies of the Johnson administration. Interestingly, while most of the adult programs mounted during the War on Poverty have since been downsized or eliminated, two of the child-centered programs—Head Start and Title I—have earned popular support and increasing shares of the federal budget. These two education programs differ in structure and in their target populations. Head Start was originated to prepare preschool children for the challenges of elementary school. Title I, on the other hand, is traditionally known as Johnson's response to educational deficiencies among the nation's poor elementary and secondary school-aged children.

Head Start's roots as a Community Action Program and Title I's base in federal education agencies are only one structural characteristic that distinguishes the programs. The development of Title I services has a history quite unlike that of Head Start, and some recurrent problems have plagued the program since its inception.

The Structure of Title I Legislation

Title I was designed primarily to expand budget allocations to the U.S. Office of Education (USOE) so that it would provide greater resources to economically deprived children. It introduced greater federal involvement in American schools. However, because education has traditionally been the responsibility of state and local governments, the Title I legislation developed a highly complex administrative structure in which the federal government, states, and local districts shared administrative responsibilities. As outlined in the ESEA (1965, § 205), the federal government would dispense Title I funds, but local educational agencies (or LEAs) were to submit program applications to the state educational agencies (or SEAs). The SEAs, in turn, would approve applications if

1. the money used for programs and projects was spent to meet the special needs of educationally deprived children;
2. the programs were of "sufficient size, scope, and quality to give reasonable promise of substantial progress toward meeting those needs";
3. the LEA would provide services to educationally deprived children in private schools;
4. effective evaluation procedures would be adopted;
5. the LEA agreed to make an annual report to the SEA;
6. LEAs would collaborate with the community action programs; and
7. effective procedures were adopted for acquiring and disseminating to teachers and administrators significant information derived from educational research, demonstration, and sim-

ilar projects, and for adopting, where appropriate, promising educational practices developed through Title I projects.

Once funds were distributed and programs were implemented, the SEAs would monitor LEAS to ensure that these criteria were met. State agencies were also responsible for reporting the outcomes of their compensatory education efforts to the federal government.

In recognition of the fact that the needs of educationally deprived children and impoverished school districts may differ from state to state and from one locality to the next, the legislation provided maximum flexibility. Congress permitted local schools to choose the educational methods best suited to achieve their goals. Funds provided under Title I could be used for hiring additional and special staff, constructing facilities, acquiring equipment, and "for all the appropriate cost incident to the conduct of a public school program that would improve the educational outcomes of educationally deprived children" (S. REP. No. 146, p. 1451). The federal government reserved the right to intervene only in matters related to administrative procedures and accountability of Title I funds. From the very beginning, however, an adherence to the notions of flexibility incorporated into the law has caused some confusion and many debates.

Changes in the Title I Law   During the early years of Title I, the USOE issued few administrative guidelines and regulations governing the use of Title I funds (Dougherty 1985). Indeed, Congress discouraged USOE from issuing any rules that restricted the freedom of local and district agencies to decide how to use their grants (S. REP. No. 634). As a result, many disparities emerged between the intent of the legislation and the actual use of Title I appropriations (Dougherty 1985). In 1969, for example, Martin and McClure noted that in southern states, Title I funds were misused to pay for educational expenses for black students that were provided for white students out of local resources (cited in S. REP. No. 634 and Dougherty 1985). Many districts throughout the nation allotted a disproportional amount of Title I resources to construction projects rather than to direct services (S. REP. No. 634).

During the 1960s and 1970s, Congress attempted to curtail the misuse of Title I funds. It enacted several measures to increase state and local accountability and imposed greater restrictions on the use of Title I grants (Birman et al. 1987; Dougherty 1985). In 1969, for example, Congress issued the "supplement–not supplant" provision, which prohibited states from using Title I funds as a substitute for local resources and forbade districts from discriminating against Title I schools in their allocations of state and local funds (Dougherty 1985; S. REP. No. 634). In 1970, Congress mandated regular monitoring of the SEAs, pressuring them to enforce the laws. In 1971, changes to the legislation mandated schools to establish Parent Advisory Councils that would participate in the planning, development, and operation of Title I programs. Finally, amendments passed in 1978 revised and restated the law extensively and ordered states to submit Monitoring and Enforcement Plans devised to ensure local compliance with the law.

By the beginning of the 1980s, the many amendments to the 1965 law had transformed the administration of Title I programs into a bewildering enterprise. In the view of President Reagan and many members of Congress, the administrative requirements had become too prescriptive and limiting of state powers (H.R. REP. No. 158; S. CONF. REP. No. 208). Consequently, the Education Consolidation Improvement Act of 1981 (ECIA) was passed to "eliminate burdensome, unnecessary, and unproductive paperwork" (§ 552). The new law was also intended to free state education agencies from "overly prescriptive regulations and administrative burdens which [were] not necessary for fiscal accountability" (ECIA, 1981, § 552). Since 1981, Chapter 1 of the ECIA has replaced Title I as the major federal effort on school-aged compensatory education. Chapter 1 retained many of the principles of Title I; it continued the federal policy of providing assistance to low-income, educationally deprived children, but it changed many of the administrative details and eliminated the Parent Advisory Councils and many evaluation requirements.

Who Is Targeted for Title I/Chapter 1 Services? Title I/Chapter 1 policies have always contained specific targeting rules. Funds are allotted to "economically deprived" school districts for the purpose of providing services to the most "educationally deprived students," including preschoolers. According to current federal regulations, states must calculate the amount of Chapter 1 funds each county should receive by using a formula that accounts for the average amount the state spends on each pupil and the number or percentage of children, aged five to seventeen, from families with incomes below the poverty level. The formula also accounts for the number of children who are in families receiving Aid to Families with Dependent Children payments that exceed the current census poverty level, and the number of neglected and delinquent children who reside in institutions for over thirty days (U.S. Department of Education 1990a). Finally, the U.S. secretary of education determines each state's grant allocation on the basis of the eligibility data calculated by the states.

Because Title I/Chapter 1 was designed to aid the counties and children "in most need" of supplemental education services, states must distribute the funds to the districts with the highest concentration of poverty. LEAs, in turn, must allocate their funds to the most impoverished project areas and schools (see U.S. Department of Education 1990a, 51–58, for exact procedure). Finally, the schools must guarantee that Chapter 1 services are provided to their most educationally deprived students.

The federal regulations define "educationally deprived" children as those "whose educational attainment is below the level that is appropriate for children their age" (Financial assistance . . ., 1990, 427). The law, therefore, requires that the LEAs conduct an annual assessment of the educational needs of all children living in areas targeted for Chapter 1 funds. The LEAs must also collect data on the academic performance of all children enrolled in public and private schools and in local institutions for neglected and delinquent children. Although the Federal Department of Education (DOE) recommends that standardized measures be used to identify educationally deprived children, the law does not specify which tests must be administered. Consequently, there is much variability in the actual achievement measures used by LEAs to make funding decisions. This diversity may account for much of the variation that exists from one state to another in the achievement scores of children who enter the program.

In general, as mandated by the law (Augustus F. Hawkins-Robert T. Stafford Elementary and Secondary School Improvement Amendments 1988, § 1014(b); Education Amendments 1978, § 124 (b); U.S. Department of Education 1990a), school districts use a psychometrically valid achievement measure of some sort and select children whose scores fall below a certain cutoff score (Gaffney & Schember 1982). Although schools usually select children whose scores fall below the 50th percentile (H.R. Serial No. 100-F), the actual cutoff may vary across districts depending on the amount of funds available and the particular needs of the specific children. In some instances, a child may be selected on the basis of teacher recommendations (Gaffney & Schember 1982). Because Chapter 1 funds are intended as a supplement to state funds, children who are served by other special education programs—for example, state compensatory programs—may be excluded from Chapter 1 services.

Because each state's "poorest" districts and "lowest achieving" children are relative assessments, there is some variability in the characteristics of the school districts that receive Chapter 1 funding. In general, Chapter 1 students are more likely than students nationwide to reside in districts with the highest poverty rates. According to the latest federal assessment (Birman et al. 1987), 45 percent of all Chapter 1 students are in high-poverty areas, while only 9 percent of Chapter 1 students reside in districts with low poverty rates. But it is possible for Chapter 1 recipients who are in high-poverty areas to be overlooked for services. Thirteen percent of elementary schools in the highest poverty-stricken districts do not receive Title I/Chapter 1 funding (Birman et al. 1987). On the other hand, approximately 57 percent of elementary schools located in the nation's richest districts are funded. Overall, the DOE estimates that 42 percent of all children reached by Chapter 1 are poor. The remaining 58 percent are not poor but are considered to be educationally deprived compared to others in their locale (Sinclair & Guttman 1990).

The achievement levels of students selected for Chapter 1 services also vary considerably across districts, schools, and grade levels (Birman et al. 1987). Because Chapter 1 funds are spent on the most "educationally deprived" children residing in each program district, population differences dictate how poor a child's school performance must be to make him or her eligible for services. Some school districts may have sufficient funds for all students who achieve below the 50th percentile, while districts with large numbers of low achievers may be able to provide services only to children scoring below the 25th percentile. Most students who fall below the 25th percentile on school administered achievement tests do receive Chapter 1 services. Nevertheless, a certain proportion of eligible students throughout the country do not receive Chapter 1 services even though they fall into the category of the "educationally needy." (Some of these students may be enrolled in state-financed compensatory programs, making them ineligible for Chapter 1.) There is also evidence indicating that some Chapter 1 participants score at or above the 50th percentile (Birman et al. 1987). One reason for these differences may be that federal regulations (ECIA,

Amendments 1983; S. REP No. 222; U.S. Department of Education 1990a) allow many school districts to concentrate their services on a limited number of schools and a limited number of school grades, which may restrict or broaden the range of achievement norms from which target children are selected.

Because of these variations in income and educational need among Chapter 1 recipients, opponents of the program have charged that "many children who are neither poor nor underachieving receive services" (cited in H.R. Serial No. 100-F), while many poor, low-achieving children do not. Congress (H.R. Serial No. 100-F) and the DOE (1990a) acknowledge that funds are insufficient to serve all educationally deprived children. However, they are quite confident that the current practices represent the best method of ensuring that Chapter 1 services generally reach the children "most in need" of them (H.R. Serial No. 100-F). Despite congressional claims, in many ways the current targeting process is self-contradictory; Chapter 1 attempts to reach both children from low-income families and low-achieving children regardless of their family incomes. Arguably, the current practices allow for expenditures of large amounts of money on children who do not need the services.

President Johnson originally conceived of Title I as a program that would specifically benefit economically disadvantaged children. In the 1960s these children resided in environments with limited educational opportunities and resources that could contribute to their development (Deutsch 1967; Havighurst 1966). In the 1990s the situation for economically disadvantaged children remains bleak (see Wilson for an example, 1987). Currently, children from the poorest families and communities are at highest risk for academic failure (Ralph 1989; Wilson 1987). However, this group of disadvantaged children also shows the greatest increase in achievement when adequate financial support and academic resources are provided (Alexander, Entwisle, & Thompson 1987; Ralph 1989). Every dollar that is spent on

children who are not both economically *and* educationally impoverished is a dollar not given to children in genuine need and
with veritable potential for academic attainment.

Chapter I Services

Recipients The five million recipients of Chapter 1 services in
1987–88 comprised 10 percent of all elementary and secondary
school children, including pupils enrolled in private schools.
According to estimates provided by the DOE (Sinclair & Guttman 1990), in 1987–88, 71 percent of Chapter 1 students were
in grades one through six, 16 percent were in grades seven
through nine, and only 5 percent of all students enrolled in
Chapter 1 were in grades ten through twelve. An additional 8
percent of the children reached by Chapter 1 were in preschool
and kindergarten programs. Evidently, Chapter 1 funds are
used to provide support primarily to elementary schools.

A large proportion of Chapter 1 students live in large school
districts within urban areas (Birman et al. 1987). Most Chapter
1 recipients are white (43 percent). Black and Latino students
comprise 28 percent and 25 percent, respectively, of Chapter 1
recipients (Sinclair & Guttman 1990). These groups, however,
represent only 15 percent and 8 percent of the school-age population and are, therefore, overrepresented in Chapter 1 programs (Birman et al. 1987).

Instructional Programs Chapter 1 provides remedial reading
programs to 74 percent of its students, while 46 percent receive
help with math. A small percentage of Chapter 1 children receive instruction in language arts and English as a second language. These percentages are based on program offerings at
the national level and do not describe how Chapter 1 funds are
applied in individual schools. The DOE has identified five basic
types of Chapter 1 instructional programs (Birman et al. 1987;
Dougherty 1985):

1. *In-class projects* provide instruction in the regular classroom. Children who receive in-class services are, for example, assisted in math by an aide while the other children in the same classroom are taught by the teacher.
2. *Pull-out programs* require that the child leave his or her regular classroom to receive Chapter 1 services. These are classified as one of two types—extended or limited—depending on the length of regular instruction time a Chapter 1 recipient will miss.
3. *Replacement programs* provide students with Chapter 1 services in self-contained settings during a time when they would normally be receiving regular classroom instruction.
4. *Add-on programs* provide instruction during times when students would not normally be in school (i.e., after school or during the summer).
5. *School-wide programs* that serve all students may be established in schools with at least 75 percent of low-income students.

Even this schematic list is deceptively simple. The approximately fourteen thousand school districts that receive Chapter 1 funds have unique programs structured to meet their local needs (U.S. Department of Education 1990c). The DOE uses the above categories to simplify their analysis of Chapter 1, but this classification does not capture the extreme variability in programs across the nation.

According to the most recently published estimates, the majority of Chapter 1 recipients are in pull-out programs; 89 percent of school districts provided math or English instruction in limited pull-out programs in 1985–86 (Birman et al. 1987). This percentage, however, varies across grade levels. Elementary schools, for example, are more likely than middle or secondary schools to use pull-out methods of instruction (Birman et al. 1987).

Characteristics shown to be important predictors of effective schooling are contained in varying degrees within Chapter 1 programs. The programs are generally characterized by smaller student groups and increased instructional time, and they offer more direct instruction than regular classrooms (Birman et al. 1987). However, because each district designs its own programs, the degree to which programs incorporate any of these features varies widely. For example, although Chapter 1 classes consist of an average of five students, 50 percent of Chapter 1 reading groups have three to seven pupils, 25 percent have fewer than three students, and another 25 percent have seven or more students (Birman et al. 1987).

There are also many factors associated with Chapter 1 instructional services that may limit the progress of participants. Although they receive a ten- to fifteen-minute increase in instruction time per day, 42 percent of Chapter 1 teachers report that students miss some instruction in another academic subject when they are in Chapter 1 (Birman et al. 1987). More significantly, observations suggest that many school officials design Chapter 1 programs that are consistent with their preferred teaching practices, which may not help students whose low achievement indicates they have not benefited from those practices. Programs are also designed to be amenable to state testing programs (see Birman et al. 1987), so the curricula often focus on lower-order skills that can be easily measured. Consequently, many Chapter 1 students practice repetitive drills in reading and mathematics (Allington 1990; Birman et al. 1987) but are not taught how to apply these skills. In Chapter 1 classes, as in many other programs for disadvantaged children, the teachers fragment the subject into manageable parts that children must then practice. Yet mastery of the individual steps does not guarantee mastery of the whole; these children may learn to read words aloud and compute numbers, but if they have few opportunities to engage in the higher-order skills entailed in reading a full text or in applying mathematical facts to problem solving (Birman et al. 1987), the purpose of this learning is nullified. When Chapter 1 children receive tutoring that is elementary and less challenging than the instruction provided in the regular classroom, the achievement gap between disadvantaged children and their more privileged peers will not be narrowed and the goals of Chapter 1 never realized.

The Effects of Title I/Chapter I on Student Achievement

The Title I/Chapter 1 law has always featured an evaluation component (see ESEA 1965, § 205(a)(5)). However, a review of the legislative histories suggests that, despite the legal prescriptions, evaluation of the effectiveness of Chapter 1 services has not always been a priority of policymakers and program developers. The Title I Evaluation and Reporting System (TIERS) was not developed until the mid-1970s as a formal procedure requiring states to submit specific information about their programs to the federal government (Education Amendments 1974, § 151; Education Amendments 1978, § 124(g) and § 183; Kennedy, Birman, & Demaline 1986). Prior to 1979, however, evaluation requirements were not enforced, and states were not obligated to prepare reports uniformly. During the 1979–80 school year, each SEA began to use TIERS to compile reports about Chapter 1 projects and the students receiving services from all—or in some cases a representative sample—of its school districts. The standardized format of TIERS allowed the DOE to aggregate state reports and to develop a national summary of achievement scores (Kennedy, Birman, & Demaline 1986). But evaluation held such a low priority for the Reagan administration that in 1981, ECIA Chapter 1 repealed the authorization for TIERS. According to reports compiled by the DOE (Kennedy, Birman, & Demaline 1986, D-9), the last "mandatory data collection and reporting of evaluation data occurred in the last three years of Title I (1979–80, 1980–81, and 1981–82)."

Amendments to ECIA in 1983 reinstated some of the evaluation requirements (ECIA Amendments 1983, §1(b); H.R. REP. No. 51), yet "since the enactment of ECIA, collection, analysis, and reporting based on TIERS have been voluntary" (Kennedy,

Birman, & Demaline 1986, D-9). Most states have continued to submit achievement data, but each state does not necessarily report comparable information or data for all grades (Sinclair & Guttman 1990). The standard Title I reporting format currently used by states lists only how many children have participated in services, number tested, posttest scores, normal curve equivalent scores (NCE), and NCE gain scores. Because the yearly reporting system does not include information about instruction practices, it is not possible to determine which programs have contributed to the increases in posttest scores.

When policymakers have shown a serious interest in evaluations (Education Amendments 1974, § 151; Education Amendments 1978; ECIA Amendments 1983), the national assessments of Chapter 1 have been highly constrained by the methodological inadequacies of the investigations (Carter 1984; see H.R. Serial No. 100-F and Birman et al. 1987 for a critique of the Carter study; Kennedy, Birman, & Demaline 1986; Kennedy, Jung, & Orland 1986) and the variability in programs. Because each school district designs a unique instructional program, it has been difficult to assess the overall achievement gains of participants and to identify clearly which outcomes have been achieved and the factors that have contributed to observed gains. Consequently, researchers have confined their investigations to the academic areas most enriched by Chapter 1 programs— English and math—and have concentrated primarily on the impact of services on standardized tests scores (Birman et al. 1987; Kennedy, Birman & Demaline 1986; Kennedy, Jung, & Orland 1986).

Different results have been achieved by instructional programs in math as compared to programs in English. While Chapter 1 students tested in reading during the 1987–88 academic year showed pretest to posttest increases of 2 to 5 percentile points, those tested in mathematics showed increases of 3 to 11 percentile scores (Sinclair & Guttman 1990). Variations also exist across age groups, with larger gains occurring among children who receive Chapter 1 services during the elementary grades. In mathematics, the most significant posttest increases were found among students in grades two through six. These children demonstrated increases of 7 to 11 percentiles, while students in grades nine to eleven showed increases of only 3 to 4 percentiles, and those in grade twelve actually decreased one percentile rank.

Overall, assessments of Chapter 1 have shown that the programs elevate academic achievement, but these changes are minimal and do not place students above the 50th percentile rank. During the 1987–88 school year, posttest percentiles on reading tests ranged from 21 for high school seniors to 27 for children in grades two, four, and six; in mathematics the posttest percentiles ranged from 27 to 31 for high school participants and from 30 to 38 for children in elementary school (Sinclair & Guttman 1990). Clearly, Chapter 1 programs have not decreased the disparity in the achievement levels of economically deprived students and their more advantaged peers (Birman et al. 1987; Kennedy, Birman, & Demaline 1986; Kennedy, Jung, Orland 1986; Plunkett 1985; Ralph 1989). There is also very strong evidence suggesting that any achievement gains obtained during Chapter 1 participation are not sustained when students stop receiving the services (Birman 1988; Birman et al. 1987; Kennedy, Birman, & Demaline 1986; Mullin & Summers 1983; Rosenberg 1988).

Title I was designed in the hope that additional spending on education would offset the expense of providing occupational training and maintaining correctional facilities, and would improve the nation's military and economic prowess (S. REP. No. 146). Since 1965, the United States has spent approximately $70 billion (National Center for Education Statistics 1981, 1987, 1989) on Title I/Chapter 1 services. However, because no adequate assessments have been made of the dropout rates, employment records, or delinquent activity of the participants (Birman et al. 1987; Kennedy, Birman, & Demaline 1986; Kennedy,

Jung, & Orland 1986), it is uncertain whether spending on Title I programs has offset spending in these areas. Clearly, limiting assessments to test scores is insufficient. The existing evaluation reports provide no information regarding performance of the very skills that are necessary for success outside of the classroom. To date, no comprehensive information about the impact of Title I/Chapter 1 services on children's higher-order skills, for example, written composition and abstract problem solving, is available. Because of the lack of longitudinal data, it is not possible to talk about the impact on students' future education and employability (Birman et al. 1987).

Conclusions

Unlike those of Head Start, the goals of Title I/Chapter 1 are not clear. The federal government distributes monies to states so that they may alleviate the consequences of economic deprivation but does not articulate its priorities. Title I/Chapter 1 monies are dispersed in various ways to various demographic groups and various programs. Exactly which of the factors associated with academic underachievement does the nation want to address? It is time to reflect on America's current educational needs and what we expect from the significant expenditure on Chapter 1 services.

Recent legislation (Augustus F. Hawkins–Robert T. Stafford Amendments 1988; 1992 Assessment of the Chapter 1 Act 1990; H.R. REP. No. 404) has attempted to improve Chapter 1 and expand parental involvement in the programs. Another national assessment of Chapter 1 administrative regulations, state compliance with the law, and the impact of services on children's educational achievement has been called for, and a ten-year longitudinal study will be conducted to "assess the impact of Chapter 1 on a wide variety of pupil characteristics and experiences through age 18, with follow-up surveys through age 25"(Augustus F. Hawkins–Robert T. Stafford Amendments 1988,

§ 1461; H.R. REP. No. 404). These plans are promising, but one must wonder whether they have been introduced too late and whether any significant change will arise from them.

Initial results of the national assessment suggest in fact that little progress has been made since the enactment of the 1988 legislation. The Hawkins-Stafford amendments focused on assessing the effectiveness of Chapter 1 projects and required that all projects which did not meet the minimum standards of effectiveness established by the state develop program improvement plans aimed at increasing student achievement. But, according to a report issued by the U.S. Department of Education, "Chapter 1 program improvement is a 'non-event' in many schools identified as in need of improvement. The improvement plans and activities implemented to date are modest at best" (1992, 44). Congress intended that Chapter 1 programs adopt and continue to implement improvement plans when students did not show gains in achievement, but these have not been undertaken and no penalties have been incurred by programs that have failed to increase achievement. The obvious reason for sidestepping the intent of the law is that failure of a Chapter 1 program does not lead to a diminishment of funds or other tangible consequences (U.S. Department of Education 1992).

The improvement amendments also encourage schools to implement and adopt successful Chapter 1 and non–Chapter 1 programs. In this vein, the mandated evaluation includes studies aimed at identifying successful implementation strategies and providing descriptions of what is required to replicate programs that have proven effective in increasing the academic achievement of participants. But these mandates are not necessarily accompanied by committed assistance. The Secretary's Initiative and the Diffusion Network (evaluation programs set up during the 1970s to investigate and disseminate information about programs with proven effectiveness) still exist but are too poorly funded to help SEAs, LEAs, and schools discover which programs would best serve their needs.

Title I/Chapter 1 has been implemented for nearly thirty years, but the achievement of the nation's disadvantaged students continues to be poor. Do we really want to continue offering them more of the same and hope that somehow we will begin to see better results? Clearly it is time to demand accountability to justify this significant expenditure of tax dollars. We must begin to truly experiment with the program so that Chapter 1 participants can finally receive the help they need and deserve in order to succeed.

References

1992 Assessment of Chapter 1 Act, Pub. L. No. 101–305, 104 STAT. 253. 1990.

Alexander, K., D. R. Entwisle, & M. S. Thompson. 1987. School performance and status relations. *American Sociological Review* 52:665–82.

Allington, R. L. 1990. Effective Literacy Instruction for at-risk children. In M. S. Knapp & P. M. Shields, eds., *Better schooling for the children of poverty: Alternatives to conventional wisdom,* 2:13–19. Menlo Park, Calif.: SRI International.

Augustus F. Hawkins–Robert T. Stafford Elementary and Secondary School Improvement Amendments of 1988, Pub. L. No. 100–297, 102 STAT. 130. 1989.

Birman, B. 1988. How to improve a successful program: Pointers from the National Assessment of Chapter 1. *American Educator* 12:22–29.

Birman, B. F., M. E. Orland, R. K. Jung, R. J. Anson, & G. N. Garcia. 1987. *The current operation of the Chapter 1 program.* Washington, D.C.: U.S. Department of Education.

Campbell, D. T. 1969. Reforms as experiments. *American Psychologist* 24:409–29.

Carter, L. F. 1984. The Sustaining Effects Study of Compensatory and Elementary Education. *Educational Researcher* 13(7):4–13.

Coleman, J. S., E. Q. Campbell, C. J. Hobson, J. McPartland, A. M. Mood, F. D. Weinfeld, & R. L. York. 1966. *Equality of educational opportunity.* Washington, D.C.: U.S. Government Printing Office.

Deutsch, M. 1967. The disadvantaged child and the learning process.

In M. Deutsch, ed., *The disadvantaged child,* 49–57. New York: Basic Books.

Dougherty, J. C. 1985. *A matter of interpretation: Changes under Chapter 1 of the Education Consolidation and Improvement Act,* House Committee on Education and Labor, H.R. Doc. Serial No. 99-B, 99th Cong., 1st Sess.

Education Amendments of 1974. Pub. L. No. 93–380, § 151, 88 STAT. 484 (1974).

Education Amendments of 1978. Pub. L. No. 95–561, 92 STAT. 2143 (1978).

Education Consolidation and Improvement Act of 1981 (ECIA), Pub. L. No. 97-35, 95 STAT. 463 (1981).

Education Consolidation and Improvement Act of 1981 (ECIA), Amendments, Pub. L. No. 98-211, 97 STAT. 1412, (1983).

Elementary and Secondary Education Act of 1965 (ESEA), Pub. L. No. 89-10, 1965 U.S. CODE CONG. & ADMIN. NEWS (79 STAT.) 27.

Financial assistance to local educational agencies to meet special educational needs of disadvantaged children, 34 C.F.R. § 200.6 (1990).

Gaffney, M. J., & D. M. Schember. 1982. *Current Title I school and student selection procedures and implications for implementing Chapter 1, ECIA.* McLean, Va.: Advanced Technology, Inc.

H.R. REP. 158, 97th Cong., 1st Sess., reprinted in 1981 U.S. CODE CONG. & ADMIN. NEWS, 1010.

H.R. REP. 404, 101st Cong., 2nd Sess., reprinted in 1990 U.S. CODE CONG. & ADMIN. NEWS 214.

H.R. REP. 51, 98th Cong., 1st Sess., reprinted in 1983 U.S. CODE CONG. & ADMIN. NEWS, 2188.

H.R. Serial No. 100-F, 100th Cong. (1987).

Hale, B. A., V. Seitz, & E. Zigler. 1990. Health services and Head Start: A forgotten formula. *Journal of Applied Developmental Psychology,* 11:447–58.

Harrington, M. 1962. *The other America: Poverty in the United States.* New York: Macmillan.

Havighurst, R. 1966. Who are the socially disadvantaged? In S. Webster, ed., *The disadvantaged learner,* 20–29. San Francisco: Chandler.

Jencks, C. 1986. Comment on Education and Training Programs and Education. In S. H. Danziger & D. H. Weinberg, eds., *Fighting poverty.* Cambridge: Harvard University Press.

Kennedy, M. M., B. F. Birman, & R. E. Demaline. 1986. *The effectiveness* of Chapter 1 services. Washington, D.C.: U.S. Department of Education.

Kennedy, M. M., R. K. Jung, & M. E. Orland. 1986. Poverty, achievement and the distribution of compensatory education services. Washington, D.C.: U.S. Department of Education.

Kirschner Associates. 1970. A national survey of the impacts of Head Start centers on community institutions. Washington, D.C.: Office of Economic Opportunity.

Knapp, M. S., & P. M. Shields. 1990. Better schooling for the children of poverty: Alternatives to conventional wisdom. Vol. 2. Menlo Park, Calif.: SRI International.

McKey, R., L. Condelli, H. Ganson, B. Barrett, C. McConkey, & M. Plantz. 1985. The impact of Head Start on children, families and communities: Final report of the Head Start Evaluation, Synthesis and Utilization Project (DHHS Publication No. OHDS 85-31193). Washington, D.C.: U.S. Government Printing Office.

Mediax Associates. 1980. Accept my profile: Perspectives for Head Start profiles of program effects on children. Westport, Conn.

Mullin, S. P., & A. A. Summers. 1983. Is more better? The effectiveness of spending on compensatory education. Phi Delta Kappan 64(5):339–47.

National Center for Education Statistics. 1981. Digest of education statistics. Washington, D.C.: U.S. Government Printing Office.

———. 1987. Digest of education statistics. Washington, D.C.: U.S. Government Printing Office.

———. 1989. Digest of education statistics. Washington, D.C.: U.S. Government Printing Office.

Plunkett, V. R. L. 1985. From Title I to Chapter 1: The evolution of compensatory education. Phi Delta Kappan 66(8):533–37.

Ralph, J. 1989. Improving education for the disadvantaged: Do we know whom to help? Phi Delta Kappan 70(5):395–401.

Rosenberg, B. 1988. A look forward and backward. American Educator 12:30–31, 45–47.

Rossi, P. H., & H. E. Freeman. 1989. Evaluation: A systematic approach. Newbury Park, Calif.: Sage, Inc.

S. CONF. REP. No. 208, 97th Cong., 1st. Sess., reprinted in 1981 U.S. CODE CONG. & ADMIN. NEWS, 396.

S. REP. No. 222, 100th Cong., 2nd. Sess., reprinted in 1988 U.S. CODE CONG. & ADMIN. NEWS 101.

S. REP. No. 146, 89th Cong., 2nd. Sess., reprinted in 1965 U.S. CODE CONG. & ADMIN. NEWS 1446.

S. REP. No. 634., 91st Cong., 2nd. Sess., reprinted in 1970 U.S. CODE CONG. & ADMIN. NEWS 2768.

S. REP No. 726, 90th Cong., 2nd Sess., reprinted in 1967 U.S. CODE CONG. & ADMIN. NEWS, 2730.

Sinclair, B., & B. Guttman. 1990. *A summary of state Chapter 1 participation and achievement information for 1987–88.* Washington, D.C.: U.S. Department of Education.

U.S. Department of Education. 1990a. *Chapter 1 Policy Manual: Basic Programs of Operation by Local Educational Agencies.* Washington, D.C.

———. 1990b. Cavazos announces $5.3 billion in Chapter 1 grants. News release, May 23.

———. 1990c. *Chapter 1.* Program summary provided by the Office of Compensatory Education, Washington, D.C.

———. 1992. *National assessment of the Chapter 1 program: The interim report.* Washington, D.C.

Wilson, W. J. 1987. *The truly disadvantaged: The inner city, the underclass, and public policy.* Chicago: University of Chicago Press.

Zigler, E., W. Abelson, & V. Seitz. 1973. Motivational factors in the performance of economically disadvantaged children on the Peabody Picture Vocabulary Test. *Child Development* 44:294–303.

Zigler, E., W. D. Abelson, P. K. Trickett, & V. Seitz. 1982. Is an intervention program necessary in order to improve economically disadvantaged children's IQ scores? *Child Development* 53:340–48.

Zigler, E., & J. Freedman. 1987. Early experience, malleability, and Head Start. In J. J. Gallagher, ed., *The malleability of children,* 85–95. Baltimore: Paul H. Brookes.

Zigler, E., & V. Seitz. 1982. Head Start as a national laboratory. *The Annals of the American Academy of Political and Social Science* 461:81–90.

Zigler, E., & J. Valentine, eds. 1979. *Project Head Start: A legacy of the War on Poverty.* New York: Free Press.

Chapter 4 ■ The Head Start Transition Project: Head Start Goes to Elementary School

EDWARD M. KENNEDY

Head Start's twenty-fifth anniversary was celebrated recently with legislation authorizing a landmark $20 billion expansion of the comprehensive preschool program over the next four years. By 1994, Head Start should be available to every eligible three-, four-, and five-year-old child in the nation. In addition, funds were set aside to enhance the quality of the program through increased staff salaries and improved training, transportation, and facilities. Despite the high price tag of the legislation, which would increase the program fivefold during a time of great concern over the budget, the Head Start Expansion and Improvement Act passed both Houses of Congress almost unanimously (Human Services Reauthorization Act of 1990). Advocates for the bill included a diverse assembly of children's experts, state and local officials, educators, antipoverty organizations, unions, and business leaders. After a quarter century of success, Head Start came of age with broad support for its continued expansion.

Consensus for expanding Head Start grew because of its strong track record, demonstrated through ample evidence and research. Early childhood intervention has been credited with increasing children's chances of becoming literate, graduating from high school, and going on to college or employment. At the same time, intervention decreases children's chances of requiring special education, becoming pregnant as teenagers, or having a run-in with the law. These findings are compiled from longitudinal studies of Head Start and many other early intervention efforts. For one of these projects, the Perry Preschool Program, scientists at the High/Scope Educational Research Foundation estimated that every dollar invested in high quality early childhood education saves up to six dollars in future costs (Weikart 1989). As a result, Head Start has tapped the support of individuals and organizations concerned with achieving education reform, empowering families to become self-supporting, and restoring the competitiveness of American industry.

Head Start's success derives from several critical components. First, program performance standards require the use of a developmentally appropriate curriculum keyed to each child's needs and to all areas of the child's development. Through such a program, teachers facilitate, rather than direct, learning. By making individual choices about their activities, children build a disposition for learning and creative problem solving. In the same manner, the program provides opportunities that foster social and emotional development, because the child needs more than academic skills to be competent in school and in life. Second, Head Start provides a range of support services, including health, dental, mental health, social services and nutrition, as well as services for families, such as education and training for parents. Finally, Head Start is known for its extensive parent involvement, ranging from parent volunteers in the classroom to parental roles in setting center policies.

The challenge in the next quarter century is to build upon these components to make Head Start even more effective. The new legislation included authorizations for a longitudinal study exploring the manner in which Head Start's benefits are achieved for specific subpopulations of children. In addition, in response to concerns that certain populations of children need longer-term intervention, the legislation provided funding for pilot programs to serve children from birth to age five (traditional Head Start programs begin at age three or four) and to serve former Head Start children from kindergarten through grade three. The latter program, known as the Head Start Transition Project, authorizes $20 million in grants to fund at least one demonstration site in each state for three years. An evaluation of the projects and their effects is also included in the legislation.

The Transition Project holds particular promise for enabling children to maintain the gains they have made in Head Start. Head Start is not an "inoculation" against school failure; instead, it is a foundation for a continuous program of comprehensive services for disadvantaged children. Although long-term gains result from Head Start, its benefits are clearest in the years immediately following program participation (Balasubramaniam & Turnbull 1988). To reap the full advantage of the national investment in Head Start, we must protect it in the elementary school years. Accordingly, the Transition Project provides funding for Head Start agencies and public schools to work together to incorporate critical elements of Head Start into the elementary school program. If successful, it will improve the way in which elementary schools serve not just former Head Start students, but all children.

Design of the Transition Project

Head Start and elementary schools often employ different approaches to at-risk children and rarely work together even when they serve the same child. As the National Association of State Boards of Education observed in its report *Right from the Start,* "While nearly all children move into public schools from an early childhood program, very few public schools have any system for learning about this experience or smoothing the transition for children entering kindergarten" (1988, 7). The resulting discontinuity can be harmful and can undo much of what Head Start has accomplished. This concern was raised by the Silver Ribbon Panel, convened to make recommendations for the future of Head Start, which observed that "[t]here is increasing concern that the progress made by children in the Head Start program may be lost when there is not continuation of comprehensive services in school" (National Head Start Association 1990, 31).

Continuity is essential if children are to make a smooth transition to elementary school. Toward this end, the Head Start Transition Project includes three central components:

1. coordination and joint planning for developmental continuity between the Head Start and elementary school programs;
2. continuation of comprehensive support services during the elementary school years; and
3. extensive parent involvement in elementary education.

Through funds available under the Head Start Transition Project, Head Start agencies and local educational agencies working in partnership with one another to adopt these three components may receive grants from the Administration on Children, Youth and Families, which administers Head Start. Teams of trained family services coordinators will help parents, administrators, and teachers respond to the educational and noneducational needs of students. The teams will conduct home visits, help students and families obtain support services, coordinate family outreach and support, involve parents in the management of the transition program, and enhance developmental continuity between the programs. Family services coordinators will prepare a plan for the transition of each child from Head Start to kindergarten, including the transfer of records and a meeting of the Head Start and kindergarten teachers and the child's parents. To receive funds, the Head Start and public school partnership must arrange for state, local, and community-based agencies serving their students to designate liaisons to the program, and families must be involved in its design and operation.

Project Components

The Transition Project builds on the experience of earlier programs on the transition from Head Start to elementary schools, including Project Developmental Continuity (Bond & Rosario 1982) and Follow Through (Doernberger & Zigler, chapter 2), as well as programs designed to make schools more responsive to the needs of low-income children, for example, Edward Zigler's School of the Twenty-first Century (Zigler & Lang 1991), the national Cities in Schools program, and James Comer's School Development Program (Comer 1986). Most important, each component of the program is based in sound theory supported by research and experience in Head Start and elsewhere.

Coordination Traditionally, Head Start has operated independently of the public school system, with little communication between the two. This lack of coordination stems from two sources. First, public education policy involves a strong state role, while Head Start, a federal program conducted at the local level, has no state agency with which state-level coordination might take place. In some cases, states have begun their own preschool programs independent of Head Start; relatively few states have undertaken state-level early education policy that includes Head Start (Goodman & Brady 1988). Second, at the local level, Head Start is generally operated by private, nonprofit organizations with no connection to the public school system (General Accounting Office 1989). In most communities, no mechanism for coordination exists. The effects of the lack of coordination range from failure to share even simple information about children's needs to complete program duplication. Some public schools have even started their own early childhood programs, competing for staff, children, and facilities and creating resentment between school and Head Start staff (Goodman & Brady 1988).

The Transition Project, by making grants only to *partnerships* of Head Start agencies and local educational agencies, creates a financial incentive for cooperation. As public schools become more aware of Head Start, duplication of services will be discouraged, resulting in a better allocation of resources. Schools and Head Start may find ways to share resources (for example, staff training or after-school child care facilities) and information (for example, ways of improving services for low-income children). In many communities, the two agencies may find it more cost-effective to work together even if limited demonstration funds are not available.

Once the cooperative relationship is established and a transition grant awarded, the preschool and school agencies are required to work together to ensure developmental continuity. Coordination of teaching methods will minimize the disturbing disjunctions that undermine children's sense of security, self-esteem, and ability to learn. To this end, meetings between the Head Start and kindergarten teaching staffs are required. Continuity is also promoted by family service coordinators, who serve as a permanent link between the two programs and between program and home.

Comprehensive Services   While Head Start's comprehensive program, which devotes attention to health, mental health, dental, nutrition, and social service needs, is a vital part of its success for low-income children, such services are rarely available in public schools. Yet a year's experience with Head Start cannot eliminate all the stresses and problems associated with poverty. In the past decade, the number of children in poverty has increased 25 percent. There has also been a disturbing increase in the number of children with multiple risk factors that can, if unheeded, impair their intellectual, social, and physical development. Michael Kirst describes the complexities:

> Johnny can't read because he needs glasses and breakfast and encouragement from his absent father; Maria doesn't pay attention in class because she can't understand English very well and she's worried about her mother's drinking and she's tired from trying to sleep in the car; Dick is flunking because he's frequently absent. His mother doesn't get him to school because she's depressed and lost her job. (1990, 1)

A majority of teachers believe that more than 20 percent of their students have serious family problems that significantly hinder their learning in school; 89 percent of teachers believe that child abuse and neglect are a problem in their schools; clear majorities of teachers identify poor health and nutrition as a cause for concern (Boyer 1990). These problems go beyond the traditional mission of the schools but can seriously impair a child's academic progress.

Dysfunctional families and their children may benefit from various services depending on their individual circumstances. According to a Department of Health and Human Services report, they may need mental health services, housing, substance abuse treatment, education and job training, medical and dental services, parenting skills training, and/or child abuse counseling (Kusserow 1989). Such families often have difficulty accessing the help that is available. Navigating through the myriad federal, state, and local bureaucracies that provide these services is no easy task. Something as simple as lack of transportation or child care can prevent parents from obtaining helpful services even where they are provided for free through community agencies. By coordinating the provision of comprehensive services, Head Start assists some of these families in meeting their basic needs for a year, but continued intervention is needed in many cases.

Kirst recommends that an alliance of parents, social service agencies, and educators address the needs of children from dysfunctional families by locating "hubs" for integrated social services. Schools can serve this function, but more important than the location is the development of relationships within the community that foster true collaboration. Educators increasingly agree that the school's attention to support services must be extended beyond the handful of overworked school nurses and counselors typically on staff. *Right from the Start* calls for schools to

1. Participate as active members of community coordinating bodies . . .
2. Develop coordination and referral procedures . . .
3. Identify appropriate staff . . . who will be responsible for planning collaboration of child and family services in the school . . .
4. Encourage innovative family support services that build on existing community services and linkages with public schools. . . . (National Association of State Boards of Education 1988, 32)

Such "school-linked" comprehensive services are also recommended by the Quality Education for Minorities Project (1990), the Committee for Economic Development (1987), and the National Governors' Association (1987).

The Head Start Transition Project provides a foundation for these collaborative efforts. Grantees are called upon to assist low-income elementary school students and their families in "obtaining supportive services that build on the strength of families, including health, immunization, mental health, nutrition, parenting education, literacy, and social services (including substance abuse treatment, education, and prevention services)" (P.L. 101–501, section 133(a)(1)). As a first step, the grantee must develop a relationship with state and local agencies and community-based organizations that provide services and enlist their assistance in the development and operation of the program. In many areas, Head Start has worked closely with these groups, so the foundation for the alliance is already in place. Once the program is established, family service coordinators serve as case managers and home visitors, working with families, teachers, administrators, and community agencies to ensure that children obtain the services they need. If successful, new collaborations formed through the Transition Project will enable schools to extend the model to older children and to children who have not benefited from Head Start or a similar program.

Parent Involvement   Children need the active involvement of their families to achieve their full educational potential. Parents can play a positive role in the educational process by reinforcing learning at home and helping teachers understand the child's unique needs. Few government programs have been as successful as Head Start in bringing the concept of parent involvement to life. Even reluctant parents, once they see Head Start's positive effects on their children, often develop a relationship of trust with program staff that allows many forms of parental involvement. Through Head Start, disadvantaged parents— often single mothers—are able to improve their parenting skills and learn the basics of nutrition, health care, and child development that will benefit the whole family. In addition, they may receive the support needed to lift themselves out of poverty, including literacy training and job training referrals. Head Start itself offers employment and education opportunities for parents. Many parents who volunteer their services to the program go on to become staff aides, receive education in the child development field, and obtain positions of increasing responsibility within Head Start (Sorensen 1990).

Most important, however, is Head Start's ability to empower parents by giving them a policy role in the program. The resulting sense of involvement and control is described in a recent High/Scope Foundation study:

> It is clear from the data that parents perceived a sense of belonging during their Head Start experiences. Through their participation in Head Start and from their communications with Head Start staff, the parents appeared to feel that they belonged when they were at Head Start and that Head Start belonged to them. Thus we get a picture of Head Start as a forceful and effective institution in low-income communities where families often feel segregated and alienated from society and from the educational and service institutions that provide help and opportunities for overcoming poverty and its trappings. (Houlares & Oden 1990, 16)

In contrast, Head Start parents reported that they did not continue their involvement in their children's elementary schools, where outreach to parents and a policy role for families are less well developed. According to one survey, a majority of elementary and secondary school teachers feel "uneasy or reluctant" about approaching parents to talk with them about their children (Harris, Kagan, & Ross 1987, 27); yet almost 90 percent of teachers feel that lack of parental support is a problem in their school (Boyer 1990). As for parents, the lower their income and education levels, the more reluctant they are to approach their children's teachers (Harris, Kagan, & Ross 1987). As Carol Ascher has pointed out, mutual suspicion and misunderstanding between low-income parents and public school teachers are not uncommon. Teachers fault parents for "failing to provide their children with the intellectual and motivational prerequisites for successful learning," and parents blame teachers for denying their children the same quality of education they believe middle-class children receive (Ascher 1988, 110). According to Ascher, parents feel that the schools do not welcome them, and educators feel that low-income parents "have tended to be so burdened by their own lives that they are hardest to reach" (110).

This unsatisfactory relationship severely diminishes the effectiveness of school programs designed to help disadvantaged children. James Comer describes the phenomenon: "When parents sense neglect or exclusion or when their children have difficulty in school, they often send mixed messages to their children: school is hope; school is the enemy. Thus they weaken the connections between the home and school and unintentionally condone harmful student performance" (1986, 444). In addition, when schools fail to encourage parents to reinforce learning at home, they miss important opportunities to increase educational success; the "curriculum of the home" is twice as predictive of academic learning as family socioeconomic status (Constable & Walberg 1988, 434).

If they have both the necessary resources and an acceptance of the need for such efforts, schools can do more to assist mothers and fathers in their roles as parents and principal educators of their children. Accordingly, the Head Start Transition Project requires funded programs to provide parenting education; offer support services for parents as well as children; involve parents in meetings between Head Start and kindergarten teachers on the educational needs of the child; support active involvement of parents in the education of their children; and include a plan for involving parents in the management of the program. These reforms, based as they are on Head Start's long and positive experience with parental involvement, hold definite promise for building home-school relationships that will extend well beyond the child's years in the transition program.

The Head Start Transition Project also appears likely to benefit both of the educational systems that it links together. The emphasis on a developmentally appropriate curriculum may improve elementary school teaching practices by giving teachers the freedom to allow children to progress at their own rate; Head Start may also learn how to strengthen its curriculum once preschool educators become more aware of the academic expectations its graduates will face in grade school. The comprehensive services requirement brings Head Start, the school, and the community together in an empowering collaboration that should improve the delivery of services to the entire local population. Finally, the parent involvement component will connect children's first and most influential teachers—their parents—with their professional educators for a full four years; this is enough time for parents to develop a habit and pattern of communication with teachers that will continue throughout the years of school. The promise of being accepted as a partner in their child's public school education may encourage a process of greater parental involvement in Head Start as well. Ultimately, these reforms can profit all students, not just those who have had the benefit of Head Start.

References

Ascher, C. 1988. Improving the school-home connection for poor and minority urban students. *Urban Review 20:*109–23.

Balasubramaniam, M., & B. Turnbull. 1988. *Exemplary preschool programs for at-risk children: A review of recent literature.* Washington, D.C.: Policy Studies Associates.

Bond, J., & J. Rosario. 1982. *Project Developmental Continuity Evaluation, final report.* Washington, D.C.: U.S. Department of Health and Human Services.

Boyer, E. 1990. *The condition of teaching: A state-by-state analysis, 1990.* Princeton, N.J.: Carnegie Foundation for the Advancement of Teaching.

Comer, J. 1986. Parent participation in the schools. *Phi Delta Kappan* 442–46.

Committee for Economic Development. 1987. *Children in need: Investment strategies for the educationally disadvantaged.* New York: Author.

Constable, R., & H. Walberg. 1988. School social work: Facilitating home, school, and community partnerships. *Urban Education 22:*429–43.

General Accounting Office. 1989. *Head Start: Information on sponsoring organizations and center facilities.* Washington, D.C.: GAO/HRD-89-123FS.

Goodman, I., & J. Brady. 1988. *The challenge of coordination.* Newton, Mass.: Educational Development Center.

Harris, L., M. Kagan, & J. Ross. 1987. *The American teacher 1987: Strengthening links between home and school.* New York: Louis Harris and Associates.

Houlares, J., & S. Oden. 1990. *A follow-up study of Head Start's role in the lives of children and families: Interim report.* Ypsilanti, Mich.: High/Scope Educational Research Foundation.

Human Services Reauthorization Act of 1990, Senate Report 101–501, 101st Cong., 2nd Sess., 1990.

Kirst, M. 1990. Improving children's services: Overcoming barriers, creating new opportunities. Paper presented at the annual meeting of the American Educational Research Association, Boston, April.

Kusserow, R. 1989. *Dysfunctional families in the Head Start program: Meeting the challenges.* Washington, D.C.: Office of the Inspector General, U.S. Department of Health and Human Services.

National Association of State Boards of Education. 1988. *Right from the start: The report of the NASBE task force on early childhood education.* Alexandria, Va.: Author.

National Governors' Association. 1987. *Making America work.* Washington, D.C.: Author.

National Head Start Association. 1990. *Head Start: The nation's pride, a nation's challenge.* Report of the Silver Ribbon Panel. Alexandria, Va.: Author.

Quality Education for Minorities Project. 1990. *Education that works: An action plan for the education of minorities.* Cambridge: Massachusetts Institute of Technology.

Sorenson, M., ed. 1990. *Head Start success stories.*

Weikart, D. 1989. *Quality preschool programs: A long-term social investment.* Occasional Paper/Ford Foundation. Project on Social Welfare and the American Future; no. 5.

Zigler, E., & M. Lang. 1991. *Child care choices: Balancing the needs of children, families, and society.* New York: Free Press.

Chapter 5 ■ Strength in Unity: Consolidating Federal Education Programs for Young Children

EDWARD ZIGLER and SALLY J. STYFCO

Since the 1960s the American people have generously supported efforts to enhance the education of disadvantaged children. Although services for preschoolers are now enjoying the most attention, programs for school-age children receive a far larger contribution of tax dollars. The evidence is clear that quality Head Start services do improve the school success of graduates, so the expenditure is certainly justified. The academic performance of older disadvantaged children, however, continues to lag in spite of the existence of two federal programs specifically designed to help them. (A third, the Head Start Transition Project, is now being implemented.) Follow Through is of course too small to reach many poor children, but Chapter 1 services are delivered in the majority of schools they attend. The public is still willing to support the cause but has a right to demand a better return.

Why is it that Head Start has been successful while the school-age programs have produced only lackluster results? Head Start, Follow Through, and Chapter 1 were all initiated to do the same thing for essentially the same children. Political and historical circumstances differentially affected the ways and means that each program used to move toward its goal. More significant to their varying rates of progress, however, is the degree to which each incorporated the fundamental principles of successful intervention.

In this chapter the ingredients of effective compensatory education will be compared among the three programs, and the strengths and limitations of each will be noted in order to inform the direction our rediscovered excitement about early education might take. The lessons from each of these projects can be brought to the new Head Start Transition sites as they work to demonstrate how effective educational intervention can really be.

Requirements for Success

Researchers have been experimenting with early intervention programs for nearly thirty years. The field is now mature enough for us to be able to cull from the literature some principles that underlie the most salutary efforts (see National Head Start Association 1990; Price et al. 1988; Schorr 1988; Zigler & Berman 1983). The first is that the program be comprehensive in scope, attending to the many factors that underlie the complex phenomenon of school performance by providing educational, health, nutrition, and social services. A truly comprehensive program goes beyond the child to include his or her primary teacher, the family. Parental involvement is thus the second basic necessity. A broad perspective is also reflected in the third principle, that a program be innovative and constantly reexamine its methods so it can modify or terminate those that do not prove their worth and strengthen or adopt those that are promising (Campbell 1969; Zigler 1976). This principle hinges on the next, that a program be committed to evaluation so planners can keep a close watch on their progress. Evaluation is of course necessary to the program's continued existence, since funding sources generally want evidence that grantees merit their support. Of equal importance, dissemination of findings fulfills the raison d'etre of experiments in intervention—to inform the field of education about how to stimulate children's learning. A fifth principle that is now emerging is that a program provide for developmental continuity rather than offer a limited, short-term "fix" for languishing problems such as school failure or the consequences of poverty. We now examine the relative presence of these elements in the three established federal education programs.

Comprehensive Services   Head Start's "whole child" approach to educational preparedness involves the provision of academic and social experiences that are developmentally appropriate as well as health care and family support services. In general the program has been quite successful in addressing the diversity of needs in the populations served. In the 1988–89 school year, 98–99 percent of the children enrolled received medical screenings and immunizations and medical treatment if needed (National Head Start Association 1990), making Head Start the largest single provider of health services to poor children. As for the education component, the preschool program appears to help children academically at least in the first few years of school, and beyond that they do succeed in meeting the expectations of school by being in the right grade for their age, avoiding special class placement, and attending regularly (see Zigler, Styfco, & Gilman, chapter 1).

The provision of support services to families has until recently been a somewhat successful component of Head Start. Although 95 percent of enrolled families received some type of social services through the program in 1989, the National Head Start Association (1990) Silver Ribbon Panel warns that this area is becoming the most problematic for local centers. In the past Head Start has spurred improvements in community services delivery (see McKey et al. 1985), but local budgetary crises and increased demand for intervention have meant that supply falls far short of the need in many locales. The panel's recommendation that there be better coordination between Head Start and local social services in order to eliminate overlap and fill voids will be discussed later in this chapter.

Project Follow Through was conceptualized to be identical to Head Start, so comprehensive services were also part of its mandate. The first model sponsors intended to pay careful attention to service delivery but, as funding levels fell, so did their ability to provide for the range of needs of project children and their families. Later program sites focused mainly on curriculum, although some offered health services (Wang 1987). Today the project operates primarily to demonstrate innovative curricula. Although this approach may produce better ways to help children acquire academic skills, robust, long-term effects on school performance have generally not been traced to any specific curriculum (see Schweinhart, Weikart, & Larner 1986).

Chapter 1 was never meant to provide comprehensive services but rather to correct "educational deprivation." Most Chapter 1 schools have chosen to do so by offering more instructional time to children who have fallen behind the academic expectations of their age level. Remedial help at this point addresses only "the failure to acquire basic skills, [not] the causes of this failure" (Ralph 1989, 400). When children are from poverty-stricken areas, as Chapter 1 participants are supposed to be, common causes may be that they come to school hungry, have parents who are more concerned about how to pay the rent than about a straight-A report card, and did not sleep the night before because of the noise and fear of gunfire on the street. Drilling academic skills into children who live in grueling environments is an exercise doomed to fail. Comprehensive services are required to put the child into a position to benefit from school. Chapter 1 services are simply too narrow a solution to the multiple problems that interfere with poor children's learning, and it is no wonder the program has little effect on the achievement level of its students.

Parental Involvement Many theorists have concluded that intervention programs are most successful when parents are involved in the services experienced by their children (e.g., Comer 1980; Lazar 1989; Powell 1989; Schraft & Kagan 1979; White, Bush, & Casto 1985; Zigler & Seitz 1982). This was more professional intuition than empirical fact at the time Head Start was planned. Parents were to be involved in their children's preschool more because, as a Community Action Program, Head Start was rooted in the philosophy that low-income persons should participate as fully as possible in programs designed to help them. Over the years Head Start has remained committed to parental involvement, as evidenced by strong policies that have been repeated in every major piece of Head Start legislation.

The integration of parents into Head Start has benefited not only the children but the program and the parents themselves. The character of Head Start's success is that graduates display adequate social competence in the long term, a finding that is probably due not to nine months of preschool but to the improved attitudes, social relationships, and aspirations that parents gain during that time and reinforce in their children in the years that follow. The program itself has certainly been enhanced by the efforts of parents who volunteer in the classroom; over 440,000 did so in 1989 alone (National Head Start Association 1990). Thousands of low-income parents have benefited financially by receiving jobs and job training through Head Start. Over 35 percent of Head Start staff are parents of enrolled children or graduates, and many of them have received Child Development Associate credentials and have entered careers in early childhood education (Collins 1990). Parents have also gained on a personal level, reporting improved relationships with their children (National Head Start Association 1990) and greater life satisfaction and psychological well-being resulting from the supportive social network of the preschool community (Parker, Piotrkowski, & Peay 1987).

The strong positive response of low-income parents to the

first Head Start programs surprised and pleased policymakers. The legislation they subsequently wrote to create Follow Through contained the strongest mandate for parental involvement of any federal program before and since (Doernberger & Zigler, chapter 2). The law established Parent Advisory Councils (PACs) that gave parents a voice in all elements of the program, including choosing the sponsored model they wanted in their schools. Follow Through was generally successful in involving parents in the early years. Parental activism in fact saved the program when the Department of Education decided to end it. As the program has downsized, funds to provide classroom jobs and activities for parents have nearly disappeared.

The history of parental participation in Title I/Chapter 1 has been characterized by vacillating federal policies and resistance in the educational establishment. Initially, the law that established Title I paid little attention to the role that parents might play. In 1971, the law was amended to establish PACs similar to those successfully operating in Head Start and Follow Through. Further amendments passed in 1978 strengthened the parental involvement provision. Three years later the PAC requirement was completely eliminated, largely in response to educators' complaints that such a mandate was an encroachment on local autonomy and would interfere with professionals' abilities to design innovative services; there was also some fear that parents would become strong lobbyists in order to get their way (Plunkett 1985). Theoretically, parents were still to be involved in the operation of Title I/Chapter 1, but it is unclear how. Amendments enacted in 1983 required only that schools hold annual meetings to explain the program to parents and "provide reasonable support" for new activities they might suggest (Plunkett 1985, 536). The most recent legislation again contains calls to expand the role of parents.

Years of disagreement over the value and means of parental participation in Chapter 1 have left the program essentially devoid of this vital component of successful intervention. We cannot even be optimistic over the latest attention to the matter, since the law has flip-flopped so often that administrators would be unlikely to devote much time or energy to implementing the requirement on the justifiable hunch that it could be reversed by another Congress. Perhaps it could never be successfully implemented until the educational establishment clarifies its mixed feelings about the ability of parents (particularly low-income parents) to become partners with teachers and share in the educational process (Kagan 1991a).

Innovation and Dissemination Compensatory education has been described as the "greatest education experiment ever seen in the history of the world" (Arthur Jensen, quoted in Ralph 1989, 395). Certainly when the country noticed that many low-income children were having a difficult time in school, the solution was open-ended and called for any ideas at all that might make a difference. Head Start was created with such open-mindedness. The planners had a very short period of time to devise a nationwide program that was to serve over one-half million children in its very first summer (see Zigler & Muenchow 1992; Zigler & Valentine 1979). And because each program was to be responsive to local needs, the agenda had to be flexible. The result is that Head Start became a national laboratory for testing models of early intervention. Over the years the program has experimented with curricula, staff training, home- and community-based intervention, and services for younger and older children (see Zigler, Styfco, & Gilman, chapter 1). Many current programs, including the new Head Start Transition project, are the outgrowth of Head Start's continuous search for ways to improve the services offered to low-income children and their families.

When the conceptualization of Follow Through changed from comprehensive services to planned variation, the entire focus of the program became model development and comparative evaluation of the models. Sponsors were those who had innovative educational plans that were ready to be field-tested. Innovation remains one of Follow Through's strongest features, but it is also the subject of harsh criticism. Those who believe the program should be terminated have argued that after twenty-five years, experimentation should have resulted in proven methods that by now should be operating in schools nationwide. Part of the reason this has not happened is that the funds required to expand promising models to other program sites disappeared after the early years. Follow Through Resource Centers, which were supposed to disseminate effective models to interested schools, had such minimal funding that they could not serve this purpose. (Dissemination has now become the responsibility of each program.) In calling for a national clearinghouse for model information, members of the U.S. House of Representatives (1990a, 42) expressed dissatisfaction with the Department of Education for being "uncooperative" in arranging for sponsors to present their plans at Chapter 1 conferences or helping them share their "wealth of information" in other ways. Unfortunately, the clearinghouse will not materialize because Follow Through appropriations did not reach the required level. Sponsors are currently limited to dispensing their findings mainly in professional journals. Nonetheless, the field of early childhood education is in need of creative ideas, and supporters argue that this is a valid reason to allow the program to continue.

Chapter 1 had the potential to become the leading developer of educational programming not only for young children but for those in the middle and high school years. The Elementary and Secondary Education Act was passed with the expectation that schools would develop imaginative approaches to meeting the educational needs of poor children (Plunkett 1985). Grantees were given maximum flexibility in the use of Title I/Chapter 1 funds so they were free to experiment with how best to apply them. In the early years there was little scientific theory or evidence to guide them (Stringfield, Billig, & Davis 1991), so planners generally followed standard educational practices and

passed up the opportunity to reform them. Despite a burgeon-
ing data base since that time, Chapter 1 never became a testing
ground for ways to enhance learning skills in children who have
fallen behind. Instead, the majority of Chapter 1 programs offer
students more of the standard educational fare that did not work
with them the first time around. If anything, the program has
tested and proven that smaller class sizes and added instructional
time are not a panacea for poor children's learning problems,
but the Chapter 1 effort has taken few steps to find out what is.

In the absence of promising new models and data to show
their effectiveness, dissemination was never a practical effort for
Chapter 1. Since 1984, states have been encouraged to submit
their most successful Chapter 1 program plans to a review board.
Those judged exemplary are given national recognition and
dissemination. Yet there is little incentive for schools to adopt
these innovative methods because their Chapter 1 funding is
essentially guaranteed provided that they meet legal administrative requirements and show evidence that students gain—even
fractionally—in achievement level rather than lose as a result of
their participation (Fagan & Heid 1991). The Hawkins-Stafford
School Improvement Amendments of 1988 may actually be a *dis-
incentive* for schools to try new approaches with their programs.
By adopting the higher goals of recognized projects, schools risk
not meeting their goals, at least initially. Schools that do not
meet self-set standards are targeted for improvement, which can
be construed to mean they are failures (Fagan & Heid 1991;
LeTendre 1991). Perhaps the allowance of additional time and
an expansion of the program improvement workshops developed by the Chapter 1 Technical Assistance Center in Denver
(Stringfield, Billig, & Davis 1991) will eventually give administrators a greater willingness to experiment and to change.

Evaluation   It goes without saying that systematic evaluation
is the only way that intervention programmers can learn the
value of their efforts. Head Start's planners used empirical data

and professional intuition to design the first program, but they knew they were making hasty decisions and were determined to correct the mistakes that would inevitably surface (Brain 1979). Evaluation thus became critical to the development of Head Start and was built into the program from the very beginning. Over the years a large number of studies have assessed Head Start's effects on many aspects of children's lives, including intelligence, school grades, achievement levels, and health care, as well as the impact of the program on their parents, siblings, and communities. All of this work has guided the growth of Head Start, suggested new directions it might pursue, and contributed a knowledge base to the field of early childhood education.

Although the project remains committed to evaluation, this effort is not without problems. A sharp reduction in the budget for research, demonstration, and evaluation suggests that current policies are based on older data despite changes in the program and in its participants (Zigler, Styfco, & Gilman, chapter 1). Another impediment is that there is still no acceptable measure of the program's main objective—social competence. National efforts to devise a standardized measure of competent behavior have been abandoned for financial or political reasons (Raver & Zigler 1991), despite "the critical importance of these evaluations to the future of early childhood intervention programs" (Zigler & Trickett 1978, 796). One facet of competent behavior, success in meeting social expectancies, has been addressed to some extent in the more recent literature. The other facet is the individual's self-actualization or personal development as a human being, a nebulous concept that is difficult to define and measure (Zigler & Trickett, 1978). The Human Services Reauthorization Act of 1990 mandates a twenty-year study that includes some indicators of competence of the first type, for example, rates of juvenile delinquency, teenage pregnancy, welfare use, and the employment status of graduates, their families, or both. Hopefully self-satisfaction indices will be developed as the research progresses. This study should afford a good sense of the true effects of Head Start for those patient enough to wait, and will allow more sophisticated study of the mediators of these effects. For now, however, Head Start's success is proven only by the sheer volume of positive reports on various indicators of competence.

As an experiment in planned variation, Follow Through also required an evaluation component. Because sponsors joined the program to test their own ideas, it was important to examine the impact of their methods on students' behavior (although they too were hampered by the lack of social competence indices). As the focus of the program narrowed to curriculum, it became logical to limit studies to school performance outcomes. The Human Services Reauthorization Act requires expanded evaluations to show the effects of the program on children, their families, and participating schools and school districts. The act also calls for a comparison of outcomes in children who receive Follow Through vs. Chapter 1 services. Unfortunately, the minimal funding appropriated for Follow Through jeopardizes the quality of such potentially informative investigations.

The evaluation of Chapter 1 has been subject to the same wavering by policymakers as the parental involvement component. Although the laws pertaining to Chapter 1 have all contained an evaluation provision, it has been either not required or, if required, not enforced. Standard reporting procedures, which would make it possible to ascertain whether grantees were generally achieving overall goals, were mandated for only three years. In 1981 the mandate was repealed and evaluation became voluntary until the 1988 amendments. With these amendments, however, the increasingly popular concept of accountability has been applied full force to Chapter 1.

After pouring billions of dollars into the program for more than two decades, policymakers have finally decided to ask for evidence that their contribution is reaping some benefits. Outcomes, which have not been examined nationally for fifteen years, will be the focus of a multi-year longitudinal study that tracks students who participate in Chapter 1 and other instructional programs (see Plisko & Scott 1991). More immediate results will be available from annual evaluations required of each school district. The evaluations must include scores on standardized achievement tests, but the law encourages the use of other assessment tools to portray a broader picture of outcomes (LeTendre 1991). Very few states have collected more varied data, however, and there is fear that educators are "teaching to the test" and ignoring useful skills and related developmental indices that are not covered by standardized instruments (Fagan & Heid 1991; Slavin 1991). Further, while the new enthusiasm accorded evaluation is welcome, one wonders if these studies come too late to instigate change in long-established programs.

Perhaps more shocking than the willingness of decisionmakers to fund a program for years and years without asking to see results is the fact that they have ignored the results that do exist. There is not much data on the effectiveness of Chapter 1, considering the size of the program, but what there is shows that students do not exhibit a meaningful improvement in achievement levels (see Arroyo & Zigler, chapter 3; Fagan & Heid 1991; U.S. House of Representatives 1990b). The students helped the most appear to be those who are just below expected achievement levels, while poorer students remain that way in spite of continuing years of Chapter 1 services (Ralph 1989). A review of over forty reports on the program led Ralph to conclude, "Those who viewed Chapter 1 as a federal program designed to meet the needs of its constituents—school districts that receive the federal money—were pleased with the administrative evolution of the program. Researchers who judge Chapter 1 by its grander aspirations—overcoming the academic inequalities associated with such factors as social class and race . . . found less to cheer about" (1989, 396). Lacking a convincing body of evidence after all this time, one may reasonably question whether this huge national investment has purchased what it was supposed to.

Developmental Continuity   A new entry into the definition of quality intervention is the assurance of developmental continuity. This concept is based on the assumption that all stages of development are important to who and what the child eventually becomes and puts to rest the false belief that there is some "critical period" or magic age when intervention is most effective (see Zigler & Berman 1983). Further, because a child is a complex being, each area of development needs appropriate nurturing and support at each stage. In addition to assuring a smooth transition between various stages of intervention, both the whole child approach and the practice of involving parents are means of promoting developmental continuity: children grow in the physical, cognitive, and socioemotional domains simultaneously, and parents respond to and support all aspects of a child's growth for the entire period of development.

Thoughts about providing developmental continuity surfaced in the planning stages of Head Start, and it has moved in this direction ever since. Attention to the whole child and the inclusion of parents were elements of Head Start when it began as a summer program. The planners knew that six or eight weeks could not do much for a child, and the project immediately expanded to last for an entire school year. Efforts to reach younger children were soon initiated. For example, the Parent and Child Centers, the highly successful but discontinued Child and Family Resource Program, and the new Comprehensive Child Development Centers were all designed to provide comprehensive health care and developmentally appropriate learning activities to children from the time of birth, and to offer family support and opportunities for participation to their parents. Other efforts to serve very young children include the

Head Start family day care initiative and the Indian and Migrant Head Start programs.

Head Start also inspired several programs to meet the needs of children beyond the preschool years. Follow Through, of course, was spawned to continue Head Start's services through the early years of school. When it became clear that the program would remain a planned variation experiment, Project Developmental Continuity (PDC) was launched to demonstrate the original intent of Follow Through. That is, PDC programs were designed to coordinate the educational and developmental approaches of Head Start and the public schools and to provide continuous health and social services for preschool graduates and their families (see Valentine 1979). Finally, the Head Start Transition Project is the most recent attempt to extend comprehensive services into the primary grades.

If Follow Through had become the large-scale program it was originally meant to be, there would be no need for the Head Start Transition program. Although the idea was—and still is—a good one, Follow Through never fulfilled its mission of offering developmentally continuous services to Head Start graduates and their peers. Initially, communication problems between Head Start centers and the public schools made this a formidable task (see Kagan 1991a). Later reductions in the project's limited budget led to increasingly smaller enrollments. Today the small size of Follow Through means that for the large majority of Head Start participants, services are abruptly terminated when they graduate from preschool.

The shape Chapter 1 has taken allows it the potential to provide continuity in the area of curriculum alone. Over 90 percent of Chapter 1 students are in pull-out, replacement, or add-on programs in which teachers typically repeat the skills presented in the classroom, perhaps with a different approach or reinforcement strategy. They may or may not share their methods with the regular instructor so she could continue the intervention during the day. Yet inconsistencies might be created by the focus on basic skills in most Chapter 1 programs. When students return to their classrooms, where more advanced thinking skills are being taught, it may seem to them that they are studying two entirely different subjects. Further, leaving the classroom can create discontinuity in the child's day, particularly if he or she misses out on regular instruction while in the program. Recently there have been some convincing calls—including a high-placed one from the director of Compensatory Education Programs in the U.S. Department of Education—to deliver more Chapter 1 services in the classroom (LeTendre 1991; Slavin 1991).

The Head Start Transition Project: A Promising Step

The Head Start Transition Project is now under way with the selection of demonstration sites. Essentially, it incorporates the goals and services initially intended for Follow Through, with a stronger emphasis on transition. The project clearly is based on the knowledge accumulated in the early intervention field: it contains all the basic elements that have been found to characterize successful programs. It also has the potential to correct difficulties in implementing these elements. In fact, the Transition Project fulfills many of the recommendations made by the Silver Ribbon Panel to strengthen Head Start.

Improved Services For many poor children and their families, comprehensive services are needed over the long term. Children obviously require proper nutrition and medical and dental care for their entire lives. The Transition Project will continue these benefits for four years beyond Head Start, giving children more protection against common health problems that can interfere with learning. Also to be continued through the transition years is Head Start's individualized, developmentally appropriate program. Preschool and school educators will be required to coordinate their curricula and pedagogies, thereby making the two school experiences less fragmented for young learners.

Providing needed support services for families has become more difficult for Head Start and for communities, and the task will be problematic for the Transition Project as well. The number of children who live in poverty has grown in recent decades, and the problems facing their families have been magnified by increases in hunger, homelessness, single and teenage parenthood, child abuse and neglect, substance abuse, violent crime, AIDS, and other horrors. There are more multiproblem and dysfunctional families who are in need of extensive and varied support services. Efforts to provide help are being made by local, state, and national agencies, but in general these programs operate independently of one another. Coordination of these efforts can maximize their impact by eliminating costly duplication, combining resources, delegating responsibilities to the most experienced or appropriate provider, and pinpointing the areas of greatest need so priorities can be set. Collaboration of this type was called for by the Educational and Human Services Consortium, a group of twenty-two prominent national organizations serving children and families. The consortium suggested that large-scale comprehensive service delivery will be possible only through interagency partnerships in which members "realize the degree to which they are capable of supporting and enabling each other's efforts" (Melaville 1991, 4). A similar call was made by the Silver Ribbon Panel, which recommended that Head Start establish broader linkages with community human service resources (National Head Start Association 1990).

This recommendation has been embodied in the law creating the Head Start Transition Project. Each grantee must have a supportive services team that includes state and local agencies that serve the same population and must appoint family service coordinators who will serve as liaisons between the team and each child's family. In time these collaborations can be expected to improve the availability and delivery of services in the entire community (Kennedy, chapter 4). Further, coordination can enable families to obtain the help they need without requiring them to "carry their life stories around to several places" to obtain help for "multiple problems, or to receive help with multiple pieces of one problem" (New Beginnings 1990, vii, v). Finally, the duration of the transition program offers hope that families can receive support for a long enough time to enable them to overcome some problems. Head Start staff report that especially "when serving multiproblem families . . . it often takes the entire first year to get to know the children and parents well enough to provide effective services" (National Head Start Association 1990, 25). Transition staff will not have to repeat this information-gathering process, and there should be no break in services delivery.

Inviting Parents into Schools   Lynn Kagan (1991a) offers a strong thesis that parental involvement is beneficial to schools, but that it cannot be achieved until there is real agreement about its value and a shared understanding of the complementary roles of parents and teachers in the educational process. She places the burden of change on educators and suggests that they can learn from their colleagues in early childhood education who have operationalized this philosophy . An opportunity for this lesson is created in the Transition Project. Each grantee must have a plan for involving parents in the design, management, and operation of the program. The respect that the Head Start staff have for the concept is sure to pervade the planning process. Preschool personnel may also advocate for parents when both meet with school staff before each child enters kindergarten. At this critical time, "alliances forged between the parent and the preschool teacher could begin to be transferred to the new teacher" (Hauser-Cram et al. 1991, 186) and initiate a lasting relationship with the school.

There is evidence that parents who have learned to work with preschool personnel will continue their involvement when their children are in elementary school if given the opportunity. For example, in the Missouri Parents as Teachers (PAT) program, a parent education and support program administered through all school districts in the state, parents have frequent contact with a trained home visitor from the time their child is born until at least the age of three. A follow-up study of families enrolled in the original pilot programs showed that by the end of first grade, parents were much more likely to be involved in their children's classrooms and to request teacher conferences than nonparticipating families (Pfannenstiel 1989). Similarly, in the Brookline Early Education Project (BEEP) parents who had close contact with their children's preschool educators displayed the same pattern when their children were in second grade (Hauser-Cram et al. 1991). Head Start is in a unique position to teach parents to advocate for their children and to overcome educators' skepticisms, thus making home-school collaborations achievable in the Transition Project.

Creative Programming and Helpful Assessments   The Transition Project demonstration programs are originating at a time of blossoming theoretical interest in collaboration as well as transition in the early care and education fields (see Kagan 1991a, 1991b). On a practical level, recent transition efforts display a variety of models and approaches that grantees can adapt to local circumstances. For example, fifteen Head Start agencies were awarded grants in 1986 to initiate transition activities, and all centers were encouraged to do the same. A report on these efforts (see Hubbell et al. 1987; Kagan 1991a) uncovered many ideas that facilitated the transition (e.g., summer activity plans for parents to help prepare their children for the change) as well as common impediments to the process (e.g., difficulties in transferring student records and poor relationships between Head Start and school personnel). Another example is the latest report on the BEEP project, which includes "problems encountered" and "recommendations" sections for all phases of the planning and operation, and devotes much attention to the formation of alliances among preschool, school, and community agencies (Hauser-Cram et al. 1991). Thus the Transition Project planners will have some interesting efforts to study as they chart their unique courses.

Evaluations of the pilot programs are mandated in generous terms that do not put so much pressure on the agencies to succeed that they will avoid trying the new and the different. The law requires continuing assessments of how well each project achieves its stated goals, but asks for information on "the problems encountered in the design and operation of the program and ways in which such problems were addressed" [PL 101-501, Sec. 137(b)(1)], as well as information on program strengths and weaknesses. These requests appear to be aimed at gathering information about how to make transition work so that future sites can benefit from the experiences of the original ones.

A final reason innovation and continual evaluation are to be expected of the Transition Project is its status as a demonstration program. Casting the project in this light was a wise move on the part of policymakers. The effort itself was spawned from experimentation within Head Start, where a commitment to testing innovative models of service delivery has paid off well—both in terms of effective new programs and in preparing Head Start to meet the changing needs of its participants over the years. Building the same commitment into the Transition Project appears to be a proven course. Second, a demonstration program requires evaluation to see if positive changes are in fact demonstrated. There is strong reason to believe that evaluation of the Transition Project will result in convincing evidence of its success and cost-effectiveness (see below), which will facilitate program expansion. Also, evaluation will answer lawmakers' requests for accountability.

Services Continuity for Five Years of Development In the early years of Head Start, Americans naively believed that a brief period of intervention would empower young children to overcome the ill effects of continuing poverty in their lives. Today it is recognized that to be most effective, intervention simply has to last longer. Two major advisory panels convened to chart Head Start's future (National Head Start Association 1990; U.S. Department of Health and Human Services 1980) suggested extending the program's length. Both of these groups also advised that for Head Start graduates to continue to succeed, better coordination with the schools was necessary. Both of these recommendations are addressed in the Head Start Transition Project.

Reports of longitudinal studies of children who attended both early childhood and dovetailed school-age programs confirm that longer, coordinated intervention produces longer lasting gains. When a very comprehensive intervention, the Abecedarian Project, was followed by a school-age program through second grade, children continued to do better than peers who had not participated; classmates who experienced only the early intervention lost their advantage, and those who received only the school-age program did not benefit substantially (Horacek et al. 1987). An intensive reading curriculum in Success for All resulted in substantial gains for children who began the program in preschool, kindergarten, or first grade, and these gains magnified each year through third grade (Madden et al. 1991). The results were much less pronounced for children who encountered the new curriculum after first grade, indicating that continuity from one reading level to the next was essential for building program effects.

A program more similar to Head Start, the Chicago Child-Parent Centers, provided comprehensive services and required parental involvement for one to two years of preschool, kindergarten, and from one to three years of elementary school (Reynolds, personal communication). Children who attended the preschool and kindergarten did not differ from controls by the time they were in fifth grade. However, fifth graders who had received four to five years of the intervention (preschool through second grade) had higher achievement scores and less grade retention, with no fade-out evident. Reynolds concluded that the transition between kindergarten and the primary grades is a crucial time, and that at least two years of follow-up programing in elementary school are required to sustain benefits.

A few studies suggest that the gains produced by extended intervention can last into high school and beyond. Initially, Abelson, Zigler, and DeBlasi (1974) found that Head Start graduates in their fourth year of Follow Through did better on IQ, achievement, and social-motivational measures than their preschool classmates who attended traditional school programs. A follow-up showed that these graduates maintained their superiority in several areas through grade nine (Seitz et al. 1983). In another study of the Chicago Child-Parent Centers, children who attended for four to six or more years had significantly better high school graduation rates. For the overall sample, 62 percent received diplomas compared to about 49 percent of controls (Fuerst & Fuerst 1991). Among students who had seven to nine years of intervention, 85 percent of girls and 70 percent of boys graduated. Center students who eventually dropped out did so one and one-half years later than other dropouts in the school system. Finally, by young adulthood boys who had participated in the Deutschs' early enrichment program from preschool through third grade had higher education and employment status and some stronger academic skills controls (Jordan et al. 1985). The loss of the advantage for girls was attributed to a more difficult transition to the regular fourth-grade classes, where their active learning orientations were not harmonious with traditional sex-role expectations.

These studies strongly support the premise of the Head Start Transition Project that continuous intervention for an adequate length of time can help poor children succeed. They further show that to establish developmental continuity in children's programs, there must be a smooth transition between the stages of intervention. Kagan (1991a) theorizes that this requires congruence of philosophy, continuity of pedagogy, and consistency of structure—goals not readily achievable given the traditional separatism of early care and formal education. This division will be bridged in the Transition Project, as it is a joint venture of educators in the two stages of schooling. Kagan further lamented that past efforts to ease transition and promote continuity have focused mainly on curriculum or "strategic alterations" in administration and procedures. They failed, she hypothesized, because they were too short term, failed to address "ongoing systemic problems," and "lacked a guiding conceptual framework" (145). The Transition Project will last for four years, will create a new system within and between the traditional structures, and possesses a clear conceptual framework based on empirical knowledge.

The continuity that the Transition Project will attempt to achieve in the areas of comprehensive services, parental involvement, and pedagogy holds great promise for the program's success. The program represents an excellent opportunity to strengthen Head Start's contributions to the lives of disadvantaged children and their families which many decry as too short-lived. Once the demonstration programs overcome the trials of implementation, it will be compelling to move the project into the educational mainstream, where its potential can be realized nationwide.

Sorting Out the Federal Commitment to Educational Intervention

Americans and their elected officials are by now convinced that investments in programs for young children are monies well spent. To prove their commitment, policymakers have supported an array of programs pertaining to the education of poor

children. Head Start, Chapter 1, and Even Start (a family support and early childhood education demonstration program for
eligible residents in Chapter 1 districts) are only three of the
federal programs that concern preschool education; the Head
Start Transition Project, Follow Through, and Chapter 1 all
target school-age children in low-income areas. These efforts
have compatible goals and serve similar populations, yet they
are authorized by different acts, subsections, and amendments
and compete with one another for shares of the federal budget.

The confused approach to compensatory education taken in
Congress is magnified when policies are implemented at the
state and local levels. "Practitioners [face] increasing numbers
of piece-meal programs, a myriad of funding streams, and inconsistent regulations" (Kagan 1991a, 132). In many cases there
are conflicting eligibility restrictions and fiscal requirements between federal and state education programs and between these
and related social services. Sometimes contrasts in laws make it
impossible to combine programs when obvious duplication exists
or stymie efforts to link complementary services. For example,
plans to coordinate Head Start and the Transition Project with
community agencies to bolster comprehensive services may fail
if the local programs (many of which are federally funded) have
different eligibility criteria. One of the reasons that the U.S.
Office of Education wanted to terminate Follow Through was
that it targeted the same ages as Title I/Chapter 1 (Doernberger
& Zigler, chapter 2), but so does Head Start. Follow Through
and the Transition Project serve exactly the same children—
Head Start graduates. The policy mishmash is exemplified in
Section 139 of the Human Services Reauthorization Act of 1990,
which calls for the secretary of DHHS to "arrange with the
Secretary of Education to coordinate programs established under this subtitle [Head Start Transition Grants] with the programs established under the Follow Through Act to enable local
educational agencies to submit a single application for funding
under both such programs, and shall, to the extent practicable,

coordinate the promulgation of regulations that apply to such programs."

Years of legislative tinkering with educational intervention programs have obviously created a frustrating maze. Ralph's analysis revealed some painful truths: "The complicated formulas that drive [Chapter 1, Head Start, and Follow Through] have tended to diffuse their impact" and bespeak "our muddled and varied conceptions of the problem"; the entangled policies hint that "supporters have exhausted any notion of whom they mean to help . . . or simply how" (1989, 400, 396). On another level, the overlap in the programs and policies suggests that time, effort, and money are being wasted at both the administrative and service delivery levels. The time has come to take a hard look at our current compensatory education efforts, to pinpoint their strong and weak points, and to use this information to revamp our strategies for educating poor children.

Head Start: Not an Elixir   There is no doubt that Head Start has achieved remarkable success in improving the school performance and life circumstances of many graduates and their families. The philosophies and methodologies that characterize Head Start are recognized as effective and should now guide our national approach to intervention. Head Start can become "a model of quality, a catalyst for change and a source of innovation" for the entire system of early childhood services (National Head Start Association 1990, v). It assumes this leadership role at a time when it is undergoing rapid expansion and struggling to preserve quality—events that bring program flaws to the surface.

Some of the problems that have hampered Head Start since its inception still exist. The program is not socioeconomically integrated, so it cannot fully prepare children for the real world they will encounter in and out of school. Staff salaries are so low that centers are finding it more difficult to recruit and retain qualified staff (Collins 1990). This problem may be ameliorated somewhat by monies authorized in the Expansion Act. Although the act contains safeguards that prevent expansion at the expense of quality, many observers raise concerns that current quality is not as high as it should be (Chafel 1992; Zigler et al., chapter 1). Finally, there is the question of whether eligibility criteria based on family income really define who needs Head Start services. Certainly not all children from low-income families require such a comprehensive program, and some who are just above the poverty line or even higher might benefit substantially from one or more of the program's components.

As we reshape or build new educational interventions, we know how to emulate Head Start's successful model of comprehensive services, parental involvement, innovation, and evaluation. We can also learn a valuable lesson from its less satisfactory elements and avoid duplicating them.

Follow Through: Unrealized Potential   Follow Through was meant to be identical to Head Start, and better in some respects. It was to last much longer, providing a substantial period of continuity in educational and other services—long enough to sustain the gains begun in Head Start. It was to attend to transition from the preschool to the primary grades, a concept that is only now being recognized as necessary to successful schooling. Once the project became an experiment in planned variation, it was transformed into a national research center for educational tools and methods that could have informed and reformed the American school system. All of these ideas are good ones, but Follow Through never received adequate funding to carry them through. The Head Start Transition Project is a reauthorization of Follow Through's plans, and hopefully they will be fulfilled under the new piece of legislation.

Once the Transition Project models are shown to be effective—and there is every reason to believe they will be—it is only logical that the project supersede Follow Through. Yet there is one feature of Follow Through that is not in the new program but is too valuable to be lost. Over the years model sponsorship has proven to be an excellent mechanism for putting into practice the theory and knowledge developed in the academic research establishment. Sponsors have kept their schools apprised of the latest educational developments and have tested the effectiveness of new approaches through the use of empirical methods not typically applied in standard school settings. Sponsors' involvement gave impoverished schools the opportunity to update their methods and enriched entire school systems in many cases. For example, in many of the early sites Follow Through methods were adopted in regular classes (see Doernberger & Zigler, chapter 2). BEEP, which interfaced with schools only for the time of transition, "focused the entire school community on more effective applications of research to educational practice" (Hauser-Cram et al. 1991, 186).

Today "educational reform" has become a buzzword, and the type of research-action approach taken by Follow Through sponsors is a good way for schools to discover what reforms to make. Traditionally research and evaluation have been low on the priority lists of public school administrators, particularly those in low-income areas (e.g., Reynolds 1991), and this disregard has stymied program development and perhaps contributed to the perceived decay of public education. Acute funding shortages in many cities suggest there is little hope to turn this situation around in the near future. Thus the Transition Project models would be well advised to invite academics into the programs for their state-of-the-art ideas, evaluation expertise, and ability to introject research into existing program budgets.

Chapter 1: A Need to Reign in Overgrowth   When Title I/Chapter 1 came into being, schools in low-income areas "had the lowest achievement test scores, the fewest teachers of remedial reading, the highest retention rates, . . . the largest number of dropouts, the biggest classes, . . . and the oldest buildings with the most substandard facilities" (Plunkett 1985, 534). Over twenty-five years and tens of billions of dollars later, they still do. The primary reason is that Chapter 1 is a treatment program, not a prevention program. It treats a single symptom (poor school performance) of a broad underlying problem (poverty), and the evidence indicates that such a treatment is not sufficient. Another reason is that Chapter 1 funds are not targeted very effectively. Although its budget is huge, the money is apportioned to most schools in America to serve students in all grades including preschool. The funds are spread so thinly it is no wonder that, according to the chief administrator of the program, "Chapter 1 adds only 10 to 15 minutes of extra instruction per day in a given subject" (LeTendre 1991, 580), although she notes that increased teaching time is not a main objective. It is simply unrealistic to believe that a few extra minutes can significantly raise the achievement levels of children who have difficulty with learning.

Chapter 1 does have some very strong points that can help in restructuring the nation's approach to the education of disadvantaged children. First, the program is extremely popular with elected officials, educators, and taxpayers. This base of support gives it a promising future in terms of funding. And because Chapter 1 has become a stable, permanent program, "a cadre of educators expert in teaching reading and language arts to disadvantaged children has now formed" (Plunkett 1985, 537). An administrative structure has also been developed to convey funds from the federal to state and local levels and to monitor program operations. The philosophy underlying this national compensatory education program is also sound. It is more costly to educate children who suffer the ill effects of poverty, and a federal contribution to the cause makes a statement that we care about these children because a well-educated citizenry is in the country's best interest (Plunkett 1985).

Chapter 1's targeting problems are easily corrected. Today around 80 percent of program funds are spent on children in preschool through grade six; more than half of them are "educationally deprived" but not poor (Arroyo & Zigler, chapter 3). Because "children from the poorest families and communities are the most susceptible to small variations in school quality, presumably because their learning depends so much on the resources and stimulation provided in the classroom" (Ralph 1989, 397), eliminating nonpoor children from Chapter 1 services would enable providers to concentrate resources on those who are both economically *and* educationally impoverished.

By further reducing the target population to children in the early primary grades, Chapter 1 could turn around its history of lackluster results. We already know that it is easier to impact the developmental trajectory of the child early in life rather than waiting for latent problems to grow. It also makes sense that early school experiences prime the skills and attitudes that carry throughout the years of school. Concentrating intervention efforts on children as they begin school is thus a logical course, one already followed to some extent by many Chapter 1 grantees. If the program were to focus exclusively on at-risk students in kindergarten through third grade, an effective prevention program could be built that would reduce the need for remedial services at later ages.

A model of this notion is Success for All, a program in seven schools that is funded with Chapter 1 and in some cases supplemental grants (Madden et al. 1991). Researchers at Johns Hopkins University focused the program on reading because this skill is necessary in all subjects. They viewed Chapter 1 as "the logical program to take the lead in giving schools serving disadvantaged students the resources and programs necessary to see that all children learn to read" (Slavin 1991, 588), and applied program funds to training classroom teachers and reading tutors and providing curricula materials. Children in grades one through three were taught in their regular classes with the assistance of a tutor if necessary, although some required additional private tutoring. Most children were also exposed to a balanced curriculum in preschool and kindergarten that emphasized language development. In some schools family support teams and program facilitators were hired, and parents were trained to serve as classroom volunteers. The results are nothing short of outstanding and prove that literacy for all is an achievable national goal (Slavin 1991). *Every* third grader who had been in the program since grade one was reading at or close enough to grade level to benefit from regular classroom as opposed to remedial instruction. Further, in at least one school that was able to devote relatively more funds to the program, the retention rate was reduced from 11 percent to 0, saving about half the program cost (Madden et al. 1991).

Success for All demonstrates that as an intensive and focused program, Chapter 1 can be much more effective than it is now. Providing the services from preschool through third grade creates smooth transition and continuity that have incremental benefits. It also appears to alleviate the need for special services beyond that point. Schools that were able to hire family support teams and involve parents had the most significant results. Except for the facts that the program focused mainly on reading and did not offer direct comprehensive services, it incorporated all of the elements of successful intervention—and succeeded. The involvement of the Johns Hopkins researchers, like that of Follow Through sponsors, shows that academics can be a valuable resource in the redesign of Chapter 1.

A Proposal for a Chapter I Transition Project

The evidence presented in this chapter points to a sensible course of action. We must put aside the ineffectual educational model of Chapter 1 and adopt on a large scale the proven model of Head Start. The current Transition Project is one attempt to move the valuable lessons learned from Head Start into the schools, but it is unlikely the federal government will soon find the money to extend the program to all poor children. Chapter 1 already serves many of the nation's poorest children, but not very well. Moving the Transition Project and Follow Through into Chapter 1 will create a project with nearly $6.5 billion in funding. This is enough to make a difference in the education of low-income children if it is applied effectively.

The most useful application would seem to be for Chapter 1 to follow the plans of the Transition Project. As Head Start expands eventually to serve all eligible children, Chapter 1 can continue the intervention in grammar school. Coordinated curricula and continued parental involvement and comprehensive services will then be firmly placed in the schools that serve populations below the poverty level. Further, because it would serve Head Start graduates, it would concentrate more Chapter 1 funds in schools in the lowest-income neighborhods. Students above the income standards can also be expected to benefit because Chapter 1 will no longer be basically a pull-out program but will involve teachers in all classrooms that have former Head Start students. (In Success for All, for example, teachers trained in the new reading program taught their entire classes with these methods.) Ineligible students could perhaps obtain the non-educational services of the program for a fee, a notion spelled out in the tremendously popular but ill-fated Comprehensive Child Development Act of 1971. These ideas would help to integrate federal educational intervention programs across socioeconomic class lines to a degree not currently possible.

Other benefits will accrue to Chapter 1 itself. By assuming the intent of the Transition Project, Chapter 1 will finally create an identity as a true national program with distinguishable procedures and goals. Currently Chapter 1 consists of a heterogeneous array of educational services that differ in type, delivery, and quality among schools across the country. The adoption of consistent program components—comprehensive services, parental involvement, and research and evaluation—will give Chapter 1 services a common core. As with Head Start, delivery of these components can be expected to vary according to local needs, resources, and desires. Each Chapter 1 site may develop its own curriculum, for example, and health services may be delegated to the community in areas that have adequate medical resources or delivered through the program in areas where supply is short. Instead of being thousands of individual programs, Chapter 1 sites will have a common structure and theme but vary in detail—a design that has served Head Start well over the years.

A new Chapter 1 Transition Project would address many practical and policy quandaries that seem to thwart Americans' best intentions to enhance the education of disadvantaged children. The plan would meet many of the recommendations of the Silver Ribbon Panel to improve Head Start, and it would correct many of the deficiencies evident in Chapter 1. Head Start and the Chapter 1 Transition would be two parts of a coherent federal policy to meet the needs of poor children beginning in preschool. Administration and program oversight would be much easier than with the current system of overlapping, independent programs. Based on a solid knowledge base and big enough to have an impact, this new face for Chapter 1 holds promise for truly closing the achievement gap between economically advantaged and disadvantaged children.

References

Abelson, W. D., E. Zigler, & C. L. DeBlasi. 1974. Effects of a four-year Follow Through program on economically disadvantaged children. *Journal of Educational Psychology* 66:756–71.

Brain, G. B. 1979. Head Start, a retrospective view: The founders. Section 2: The early planners. In E. Zigler & J. Valentine, eds., *Head Start: A legacy of the War on Poverty*, 72–134. New York: Free Press.

Campbell, D. T. 1969. Reforms as experiments. *American Psychologist* 24:409–29.

Chafel, J. A. 1992. Funding Head Start: What are the issues? *American Journal of Orthopsychiatry* 62:9–21.

Collins, R. C. 1990. *Head Start salaries: 1989–90 staff salary survey.* Alexandria, Va.: National Head Start Association.

Comer, J. P. 1980. *School power*. New York: Free Press.

Fagan, T. W., & C. A. Heid. 1991. Chapter 1 program improvement: Opportunity and practice. *Phi Delta Kappan* 72:582–85.

Fuerst, J. S., & D. Fuerst. 1991. Chicago experience with early childhood programs: The special case of the Child Parent Center programs. Manuscript, Loyola University.

Hauser-Cram, P., D. E. Pierson, D. K. Walker, & T. Tivnan. 1991. *Early education in the public schools*. San Francisco: Jossey-Bass.

Horacek, H., C. Ramey, F. Campbell, R. Hoffmann, & R. Fletcher. 1987. Predicting school failure and assessing early intervention with high-risk children. *Journal of the American Academy of Child and Adolescent Psychiatry* 26:758–63.

Hubbell, R., M. Plantz, L. Condelli, & B. Barrett. 1987. *The transition of Head Start children into public school. Final report.* Vol. 1. Alexandria, Va.: CSR.

Jordan, T. J., R. Grallo, M. Deutsch, & C. P. Deutsch. 1985. Long-term effects of early enrichment: A 20-year perspective on persistence and change. *American Journal of Community Psychology* 13:393–415.

Kagan, S. L. 1991a. Moving from here to there: Rethinking continuity and transitions in early care and education. In B. Spodek & O. Saracho, eds., *Yearbook in early childhood education*, 2:132–51. New York: Teacher's College Press.

———. 1991b. *United we stand: Collaboration in child care and early education services*. New York: Teachers College Press.

Lazar, I. 1989. How parents make a difference. Paper presented at the meeting of the Society for Research in Child Development, Kansas City, Mo., April.

LeTendre, M. J. 1991. Improving Chapter 1 programs: We can do better. *Phi Delta Kappan* 72:577–80.

Madden, N. A., R. Slavin, N. Karweit, L. Dolan, & B. Wasik. 1991. Success for all. *Phi Delta Kappan* 72:593–99.

McKey, R., L. Condelli, H. Ganson, B. Barrett, C. McConkey, & M. Plantz. 1985. *The impact of Head Start on children, families and communities: Final report of the Head Start Evaluation, Synthesis and Utilization Project* (DHHS Publication No. OHDS 85-31193). Washington, D.C.: U.S. Government Printing Office.

Melaville, A. I., with M. J. Blank. 1991. *What it takes: Structuring inter-*

agency partnerships to connect children and families with comprehensive services. Washington, D.C.: Education and Human Services Consortium.

National Head Start Association. 1990. *Head Start: The nation's pride, a nation's challenge.* Report of the Silver Ribbon Panel. Alexandria, Va.: Author.

New Beginnings: A feasibility study of integrated services for children and families. 1990. Final report. Available from Office of the Deputy Superintendent, San Diego City Schools, San Diego, Calif.

Parker, F. L., C. S. Piotrkowski, & L. Peay. 1987. Head Start as a social support for mothers: The psychological benefits of involvement. *American Journal of Orthopsychiatry* 57:220–33.

Pfannenstiel, J. 1989. *New parents as teachers project: A follow-up investigation.* Jefferson City: Missouri Department of Elementary and Secondary Education.

Plisko, V., & E. Scott. 1991. Planned evaluations of Chapter 1. *Phi Delta Kappan* 72:590–91.

Plunkett, V. R. L. 1985. From Title I to Chapter 1: The evolution of compensatory education. *Phi Delta Kappan* (April): 533–37.

Powell, D. R. 1989. Families and early childhood programs. *Research monographs of the National Association for the Education of Young Children, 3.*

Price, R. H., E. Cowen, R. P. Lorion, & J. Ramos-McKay, eds. 1988. *Fourteen ounces of prevention: A casebook for practitioners.* Washington, D.C.: American Psychological Association.

Ralph, J. 1989. Improving education for the disadvantaged: Do we know whom to help? *Phi Delta Kappan* (Jan): 395–401.

Raver, C. C., & E. Zigler. 1991. Three steps forward, two steps back. Head Start and the measurement of social competence. *Young Children* 46(4):3–8.

Reynolds, A. J. 1991. Schools could benefit from research. *Chicago Tribune,* Sept. 27, sect. 1, 20.

Schorr, L. B. 1988. *Within our reach: Breaking the cycle of disadvantage.* New York: Doubleday.

Schraft, C. M., & S. L. Kagan. 1979. Parent participation in urban schools: Reflections on the movement and implications for future practice. *IRCD Bulletin* 14(4).

Schweinhart, L. J., D. P. Weikart, & M. B. Larner. 1986. Consequences of three preschool curriculum models through age 15. *Early Childhood Research Quarterly* 1:15–45.

Seitz, V., N. Apfel, L. Rosenbaum, & E. Zigler. 1983. Long-term effects of Projects Head Start and Follow Through: The New Haven Project. In Consortium for Longitudinal Studies, eds., *As the twig is bent: Lasting effects of preschool programs*, 299–332. Hillsdale, N.J.: Erlbaum.

Slavin, R. E. 1991. Chapter 1: A vision for the next quarter century. *Phi Delta Kappan* 72:586–92.

Stringfield, S., S. H. Billig, & A. Davis. 1991. Implementing a research-based model of Chapter 1 program improvement. *Phi Delta Kappan* 72:600–06.

U.S. Department of Health and Human Services. 1980. *Head Start in the 1980's. Review and recommendations.* Washington, D.C.: Author.

U.S. House of Representatives. 1990a. *Human Services Reauthorization Act of 1990,* May 9. (Report No. 101–480).

———. 1990b. *Opportunities for success: Cost-effective programs for children, update, 1990,* Dec. 21. Washington, D.C.: U.S. Government Printing Office (Report No. 101–1000).

Valentine, J. 1979. Program development in Head Start: A multifaceted approach to meeting the needs of families and children. In E. Zigler & J. Valentine, eds., *Project Head Start: A legacy of the War on Poverty,* 349–65. New York: Free Press.

Wang, M. C. 1987. An analysis of the impact of the dissemination component of the national Follow Through program. In M. Wang & E. Ramp, eds., *The national Follow Through program: Design, implementation, and effects* (Final Project Report 1:153–96). Philadelphia: Temple University Center for Research in Human Development and Education.

White, K. R., D. W. Bush, & G. C. Casto. 1985. Learning from previous reviews of intervention. *Journal of Special Education* 19:417–28.

Zigler, E. 1976. Head Start: Not a program but an evolving concept. In J. D. Andrews, ed., *Early childhood education: It's an art! It's a science!* 1–14. Washington, D.C.: National Association for the Education of Young Children.

Zigler, E., & W. Berman. 1983. Discerning the future of early childhood intervention. *American Psychologist* 38:894–906.

Zigler, E., & S. Muenchow. 1992. *Head Start: The inside story of America's most successful educational experiment.* New York: Basic Books.

Zigler, E., & V. Seitz. 1982. Social policy and intelligence. In R. Sternberg, ed., *Handbook of human intelligence,* 586–641. New York: Cambridge University Press.

Zigler, E., & P. K. Trickett. 1978. IQ, social competence, and evaluation of early childhood intervention programs. *American Psychologist* 33:789–98.

Zigler, E., & J. Valentine, eds. 1979. *Project Head Start: A legacy of the War on Poverty.* New York: Free Press.

Index